Letters from the Teacher

Teachings of
The Order of Christian Mystics

LETTERS FROM THE TEACHER

VOLUME II

Teachings of The Order of Christian Mystics
The "Curtiss Books" freely available at
www.orderofchristianmystics.co.za

1. The Voice of Isis
2. The Message of Aquaria
3. The Inner Radiance
4. Realms of the Living Dead
5. Coming World Changes
6. The Key to the Universe
7. The Key of Destiny
8. Letters from the Teacher Volume I
9. Letters from the Teacher Volume II
10. The Truth about Evolution and the Bible
11. The Philosophy of War
12. Personal Survival
13. The Pattern Life
14. Four-Fold Health
15. Vitamins
16. Why Are We Here?
17. Reincarnation
18. For Young Souls
19. Gems of Mysticism
20. The Temple of Silence
21. The Divine Mother
22. The Soundless Sound
23. The Mystic Life
24. The Love of Rabiacca
25. Potent Prayers

Supporting Volumes

26. The Seventh Seal
27. Towards the Light

Letters from the Teacher
Volume II

Transcribed by
HARRIETTE AUGUSTA CURTISS
and
F. HOMER CURTISS, B.S., M.D.
Founders of
THE ORDER OF CHRISTIAN MYSTICS
and
AUTHORS OF THE "CURTISS BOOKS"

2013 EDITION

REPUBLISHED FOR THE ORDER BY
MOUNT LINDEN PUBLISHING
JOHANNESBURG, SOUTH AFRICA
ISBN: 978-1-920483-11-1

Dedication

This edition is lovingly dedicated to the Memory

of the Founders of

The Order of Christian Mystics

Pyrahmos and Rahmea

and to

The Teacher of the Order

who on earth was called

Helena Petrovna Blavatsky

"Ministers of Christ and Stewards of the Mysteries of God."
1 Corinthians 4 vs. 1

COPYRIGHT 2013

BY
MOUNT LINDEN PUBLISHING

First Published in 1924

May be used for non-commercial, personal, research and educational use.
ALL RIGHTS RESERVED

PREFACE

In spite of the many editions of Volume I of these *Letters* which have been issued, there have been frequent requests for additional letters showing how to apply the philosophy of Christian Mysticism to personal problems. This Volume II is therefore issued in response to this demand.

We wish to state, however, that altho we still have thousands of similar letters in our files, this is likely to be the last volume of such letters that we expect to publish. For, since the general philosophy of our Teachings has now been set forth in many other volumes, there will be less need for letters of philosophical exposition. The letters henceforth will deal almost entirely with private problems too personal for general publication.

The books we have outlined for the future—such as *The Symbology of Genesis, The Mysticism of Revelation, The Mystic Life of Jesus*, etc.,—will probably be devoted largely to biblical interpretation according to the Spiritual-Symbolic School which we represent. For only by a mystical and spiritual interpretation—instead of a literal, historical and materialistic—of the *Bible* can the conflicting and confusing claims of both the Fundamentalists and the Liberals be reconciled.

And in these days of unrest and upheaval, in which ideas and ideals upon which we formerly felt we could rely as Truth are being ridiculed and overturned, there is a crying need for an exposition of universal principles and verities which are eternal in the heavens and manifest through all things on Earth, which cannot be overthrown by "wars and rumors of wars," by changes of fashion in thought and religion, or by historical research, excavation of the sites of ancient civilizations, etc. Such eternal verities upon which we can rely for guidance and comfort are found ready to hand in the *Bible*, once a spiritual interpretation of its symbolism is understood. While such an interpretation of many of its symbols will be found in our other works—especially *The Voice of Isis* and *The Message of Aquaria*—we hope to treat the subject in a more systematic and connected manner in our subsequent works.

The Authors.

P. S.—For further light on different aspects of *Health and Disease, The Sex Problem, Psychic Phenomena, Karma, Reincarnation*, etc., look up these topics in *Vol. I* of these *Letters*, also in our other works, where they are treated more extensively.

TABLE OF CONTENTS

Chapter		Page
	Preface	
I	Health and Disease	7
II	Psychic Conditions	23
III	Karma	35
IV	Coming World Changes	48
V	Concerning The Order of Christian Mystics	58
VI	After Death Conditions	88
VII	Prayer	103
VIII	Communication and Guidance	110
IX	Financial Problems	122
X	Reincarnation	142
XI	The Sex Problem	153
XII	Marriage and Divorce	177
XIII	Discouragement	189
XIV	Jesus and The Christ	198
XV	Miscellaneous	221
	Appendix	239
	Index	245

Chapter I

HEALTH AND DISEASE

> "There is a physical condition with me all the time that limits and hampers me very much—It is impossible to describe this condition on paper, but whatever the change is that is taking place within me, unless I can understand and work consciously with it, I think I shall soon go to pieces and have to leave this plane."
>
> Oct 25, 1922.

Your condition is largely mental, although you do need physical toning up because your system is more or less run down. Therefore, although we advise mental treatments, we also advise you to find out if any organ is physically out of order or if there is any vital disease to be attended to. In attending to this you are giving your mentality something to build up on. In fact, it is much easier to send out the mental thought of health if you are also doing something physical to help overcome the physical aspects of the condition. Comparatively few people can think absolute health unless they have some ladder or some physical stepping stone on which to climb.

Have the advice of a good physician and then take up the following treatment: Repeat the following prayer each morning the first thing on waking. Also whenever you feel badly stop whatever you are doing and repeat the prayer. "O Lord Christ, open the door of my body to perfect health. O Lord Christ, open the door of my mind to perfect understanding.

O Lord Christ, open the door of my heart to perfect

spiritual realization." Then say to yourself very positively, "This prayer is answered. I am getting better. I cannot expect it instantly, but as the door of my body, of my mind and of my heart is opened, all three of them are co-operating to let in the vital life-giving Christ-force which shall make me well." Continue this until your sub-conscious mind takes it up and literally builds it into your body, in all your atoms and in all your thoughts.

> "My mother is to undergo a major operation on Monday. Please do all you can to help her."
> June 1, 1923.

We received your telegram safely and immediately held a service in which we held your mother in the Divine Light of the loving Christ. We know she is watched over and cared for and we feel that the operation was a successful one, as is almost invariably the case when the help of the Order is invoked.

We want both you and her to understand that she is under the loving care of her Father-in-heaven and that whatever is best will surely come to pass. It is not always the kindest thing to bring one back to the physical plane unless we know the work he or she is to do is not yet accomplished. But we always ask that the care of the loving angels shall watch over her and guard her during such an operation and keep her from all astral harm and physical danger while her immortal Soul is taken up to the higher realms and instructed in whatever is necessary for her further ongoing. We do feel that in her case this surely happened and that it is quite possible she may bring through the memory of some of the blessed experiences we know she passed through.

Health and Disease

> "Am happy to say I am well on the road to health. While the operation was a major one there were no complications and I got along as well as if it had been a minor one. On the eighth day afterward I was able to walk and sat up most of the day. On the twelfth day I came home."
> Nov. 13, 1922.

We are rejoiced to hear of the success of your operation, and yet it has become almost an old story to hear of such success for patients undergoing operations who have received the help of Those whom we invoke through our healing prayers. Nevertheless it never ceases to be a great joy to us to hear of it, and we congratulate you heartily on having come out of it so well. For much always depends upon the attitude of the patient. You are quite right in saying that it is only when the patient realizes the power of the Christ within that the Christ within or without can fully touch and correlate with the patient and bring about a permanent cure.

> "Will you kindly inform me as to the true philosophy of health and disease? Why is my body always in bondage to ill-health?"
> Aug. 9, 1923.

At the present stage of evolution we cannot expect perfect health in this body which is made up of earthly atoms, except as we obey the laws of hygiene and also let the Divine Self, for whose dwelling-place this body was made, take possession and dwell more definitely both in the mind and also in every atom of the body. Also until the whole world including mankind has reached a higher level of unfoldment, the physical body not only expresses the tendencies toward disease which are the inheritance from our families, remote ancestors, etc., but also the incompleteness and inharmonious conditions of the whole world.

Therefore we always advise that the most advanced scientific methods of healing should be brought to bear upon the subject. For those who are sincerely seeking to understand disease, both through mental processes and scientific investigation, accomplish much and are cultivating the mind to such an extent that later on it can grasp and let in the divine forces of the Higher Mind. Remember that Mind is dual; it includes both the lower mind of the animal self and the Higher Mind of the Higher Self which touches the human and should rule it, in rythmic harmony with its Spiritual Mind, but the consciousness of the average person vacillates between the two. Hence, while we are using the latest discoveries and helps of science, we must recognize the fact that these pertain merely to the physical and that by prayer and letting in the divine forces of the Higher Mind we can greatly accelerate the adjustment which will bring about perfect harmony.

We must always find out just what factor on the physical plane is bringing ill-health and rectify it. Then we must recognize that the physical measures are only part of the battle; that there must also be the prayers and belief in and touch with Divinity that can enter in and give life and force to both mind and body and bring perfect health.

> "I am affirming that my sight is perfect and have great expectations that my faith will make me whole and that my Karma shall be washed away. Will you tell me how Christ healed them, Karma or no Karma?"

May 9, 1922.

We do not agree with the idea that it is wise to make affirmations that your sight is perfect, when it is not. This is a falsehood which Nature will do its best to bring to your attention, possibly by making your sight worse for a time. Our method of teaching is to affirm that the Lord Christ is your Light, your help, and that altho your eyes at the present time are not as good as they should be, yet you trust in His mighty love and power to bring you to such an understanding of physical conditions and such co-operation with this love, that it will work through your being toward bringing about perfect sight, if it is the will of God that you should have perfect sight at this time. If not, then you know absolutely that there is some great lesson in the condition which you must learn. You can have absolute confidence and be willing to take what your Christ brings to you.

"What is your explanation of instantaneous healing of the body?"
July 24, 1922.

Many claim instantaneous healing when only a temporary alleviation has been obtained; for the trouble will recur until the cause has been removed and ceases to operate. The only instantaneous healing which persists is when sufficient atoms and cells have been spiritualized to dominate the entire body. For before the body is truly healed all the atoms which have been diseased—whether from wrong use of physical forces such as diet, lack of proper elimination, lack of exercise, etc., or wrong thinking, worry, etc.—must be cast out. Therefore, to heal any disease instantly is against the laws of Nature *unless* it is the last step in a long process, perhaps lasting through several incarnations.

After any great spiritual advance there is often a cataclysm of illness during which the body is eliminating atoms and cells which, having served their purpose during the earlier stages of development, cannot respond to the higher currents of life and consciousness which have been set up as our new standard of life. Therefore, we say to those who apply to the Order for healing—and we have had many most remarkable results from the force thus sent out—that when illness occurs they must hold the thought, and aid it in every possible way, that all atoms and cells that cannot respond to their new key-note of life shall be eliminated from the system and that new and more perfect and health giving cells shall be built in. Then through the power of their spiritual understanding they should correlate with this incoming rush of atoms and thus more quickly bring about the healing.

All acute diseases run a self-limiting course by developing in the body the antidotes which will neutralize and cure them, provided the patient's body is not too overloaded and poisoned with unexcreted waste products and has vitality enough to last through the process of neutralizing the toxins of the invading bacteria. Such cases naturally respond more quickly to all healing agencies—medical, magnetic, mental and spiritual—than chronic diseases in which the actual cell structure of the organs has undergone destructive changes. In the latter case the disease may be cured, but the organs remain permanently crippled to the extent that the mother-cells which produce the new cells have been destroyed.

In many cases the trouble is merely functional, *i.e.,* the improper working of a normal function, due to nervous, mental and psychic[1] factors. Such cases easily respond to proper metaphysical treatment. But where the trouble is due to invading bacteria or to the loss of certain metals and salts—iron, sodium, potassium, magnesium, sulphur, phosphorous, etc.—which are necessary constituents of the cells, the deficiency must

---

[1] For the psychic influence see *Realms of the Living Dead*, Curtiss. 89, 90.

Health and Disease

be replaced by their proper administration ere the cells can function normally; for altho metaphysical treatment can ease or temporarily relieve the symptoms, it cannot replace the lacking physical materials.

That many cases which claim instantaneous healing are only temporarily relieved is illustrated by a patient who applied to us for help altho she said: "I have been instantly healed by every healer who has visited the city!"

> "My son was sent to the state hospital four months after his return from France. His case was diagnosed as Dementia Precox with ideas of persecution . . . .was disappointed as the work he was called to assist in was abandoned, and he suffered a nervous breakdown in consequence."
> June 9, 1923.

Through the researches made chiefly in the New Jersey Hospital for the Insane it has been found that symptoms formerly diagnosed as Dementia Precox were really toxic symptoms due either to some focus of pus in the system (examine especially the teeth, nose and sinuses, prostate, bladder and kidneys) or to auto-intoxication due to improper diet or improper cleansing of the intestines.

These matters therefore should be eliminated before any more obscure or psychic cause is considered. And we would suggest that if this has not already been done, your son should have a very careful X-ray examination of his teeth, absolutely to eliminate any pus sacs around the roots, which cannot be done without an X-ray, as the teeth themselves may appear outwardly to be perfectly normal and healthy, yet still have pus sacs at their roots. It also occurs to us that your son may have had some physical blow or injury to the brain or some mental shock which may have reacted upon the sympathetic nervous system in such a way as to upset the functioning of the various ductless glands, whose secretions we know have an important relation to our mentality.

It is also possible that there may be some area of his brain, either of scar tissue as the result of an injury or clot, or due to trophic contraction of the vascular system in that area, which would make it so anaemic as to upset its functions. In this case a proper and careful X-ray would disclose it and then steps could easily be taken to correct it. In this connection especially have the left temporal and parietal regions of the brain carefully examined by the X-ray or fluoroscope. Also call the attention of your physician to the fact that in these cases the use of the extracts of thyroid and para-thyroid and other endocrine glands have proven of great value. If these have not been used they should be given a fair trial.

"Will you please mention my name in your Healing Service and tell me how I can receive the help."

Aug. 17, 1922.

As to considering you in our Healing Services, we broadcast the help to every member of the Order every day, but when any have sent their names and have specially asked, then their names are specially mentioned. But those who ask must remember to put aside at least a few moments in the middle of the day and sit in the Silence, repeating the *Healing Prayer* and the *Prayer of Protection*, including the protection of the whole Order. Then try to see the great Light of the Loving Christ come down like a shaft of Divine Light and radiating to everyone who is ready to correlate with it.

If it is impossible to sit alone even for a few moments about noon, then take any other time that is convenient. For if you truly want the help you must make an effort to really correlate with the healing force sent out. Also do not fix your mind on the pains and illness you wish cured. Rather try to think of the Divine Love that is seeking to help you. And in thinking of the Order as your Helper, picture the Christ as the force back of the Order. Or think of the Order as a pool of clear water and the Christ Jesus standing with outstretched arms in the midst. Then think of yourself and many others stepping in and being healed.

> "From the last lesson I see that the cause of my ill health must have been wrong thinking; also overwork and insufficient food. For it is a condition which the cleverest doctors here admit is an entire mystery to them and one for which they can find no remedy. They say there is no disease."
>
> Oct. 28, 1522.

We can understand very clearly what your trouble is, in spite of the fact that the doctors can find no disease. As you say, you are underfed and overworked, and at the same time are seeking ardently for a realization of the Christ, yet you do not seem to have the right conception of how to find the Christ.

One of die vital requirements for manifesting our True Self is a sound body, a sound discerning and discriminating mind and a perfect love within the heart. The sound body and the discriminating mind are the soil, and only as this soil is pure and free from detrimental matter can the plant of Divine Love flourish and grow to perfection. Therefore, instead of seeking to starve the body and to eat as little as will support life, remember this fundamental principle and say, "I must build a firm foundation in my physical body."

You have the wrong conception. In fact, you are

following the old medieval thought that starvation, flagellation, etc. (for we flagellate ourselves when we deny ourselves proper nourishment and try to force the mind into channels never intended for it) will produce spiritual development. But in truth it is one of the greatest hindrances. Were it not, then the whole world would not be in the condition that it is today; for more people would have been able to discriminate and to receive the instruction more perfectly from the Divine; and we would have a more virile, powerful and discriminating race of mankind.

> "I am trying hard to live the life and prepare the body to be ready when He comes. Do you think a special diet is necessary?"
> March 31, 1924.

A special diet is not a part of the "creed" of the preparation for this coming event. There is one law and it is a law for all; that is, eat what is wholesome *for you.* Never mind what anyone else eats. As long as you find your own diet is not overstimulating or that you do not over-eat or under-eat; as long as what you eat is well digested and gives you strength and power and helps you in every way to be healthy and clear-minded, then that is all that is necessary.

When anyone makes a specialty either of eating no meat or any other article of food, he is concentrating his mind on his stomach and his diet. And in no place in the Bible is this advised. We must look to the Lord Christ for our salvation and not to our stomach. Therefore eat whatever you find wholesome and convenient and think no more about it.

We have a little grace which we say just before eating which gives the proper attitude of mind, and it is this: "I am a creator. By the power of my spiritualized will I consciously gather all the forces from this food and use them to create health, strength and

Health and Disease

harmony in all my bodies." If you are in a position where you cannot eat just what you would like, then eat what is set before you, as Jesus tells His disciples,[2] and give thanks. If you find anything positively indigestible, leave it alone, but otherwise eat whatever is set before you.

> "I have been a student of . . . . for seven years and have gained much, but the healing consciousness seemed to fail me in a crisis, for I had to see my youngest daughter sicken and die. She was a sincere student and eager to be healed."
> Aug. 12, 1922.

We are sorry you had to pass through such a sad experience with your daughter. And altho we know that the . . . .is very earnest and sincere and gives out much good teaching, still we differ most decidedly from their healing ideas, for we know that in many cases the mere power of thought and prayer is not enough. The same God who gave us this power of healing thru prayer and thought also made the Earth and all that is in it. In fact, He put healing potencies into almost everything that grows, and He gave these things to man to use, not to refuse.

It always seems to us as tho we were flying in the face of Providence when we refuse to use His gifts as they should be used. Also we feel that if we absolutely refuse to make use of the physical potencies given to us, we should also refuse the physical nourishing potencies and refuse to eat, for one is just as sensible as the other.

As to the earth holding forces of healing, there is not a disease, even those of which early humanity knew nothing at all, that has not some force, herb or mineral or something, that is its cure. Mankind has not yet found all the cures, but the earth does contain

---

[2] 1 *St. Luke*, x, 8.

a cure for every ill. Remember that the divine One Life or the Christ-force which is specialized by the Creator in the herbs, foods, minerals, etc., is just as much an expression of the Divine Life-force as that aspect which is expressed through mind.

Therefore, in the case of healing we use every sensible means, every up-to-date idea, under the guidance of our Divine Teachers. At the same time we use prayers and our healing thoughts, knowing that one form of the healing potencies alone is often not sufficient, but that the one supplements the other. It is just as we would do were a person starving to death. We would certainly hold him in the Light of Truth and in prayer, but we would also feed him very carefully with physical food.

So do not let your faith or your healing consciousness fail you. God never meant us to die until we have tried in faith and love all His healing powers, physical, mental and spiritual, and yet if we are blind and refuse to do the thing which is obviously sensible, then sometimes it is necessary for us to pass through a terrible experience such as you passed through, to teach us. If God had not intended us to use all His healing potencies, He would have made a different world, leaving out the healing forces and giving to man the supreme power of healing through prayer and faith alone. But he did not.

> "In thanking you very greatly for your glorious and gracious kindness, for the ablest instruction being imparted to me, I ask the following: Jesus says 'Ye are the salt of the earth.' May I be imparted the full meaning of this?"
>
> March 9, 1923.

As to your question about salt,[3] salt is the preserver

---

[3] 1 See chapter on "The Symbol of the Salt" in *The Voice of Isis*, Curtiss.

Health and Disease

and purifier of all things. Therefore there is some kind of salt in all food be it grass, herbs, mineral substances, etc., and it is eaten by all animals. Cattle, sheep, deer and all vegetable eating animals find it necessary to have what is called a salt lick where they can go and get salt whenever they need it, for animals have a natural instinct for that which is necessary for their life and preservation. Man, however, is lacking in this instinct, or rather it has been smothered out by what he is wont to call education. Thus there are cults which say we should eat salt in excess; others which say we should never eat it.

Common salt is absolutely necessary to keep the blood fluid, hence we will find that if the blood loses its salt it becomes incapable of sustaining life and produces various forms of illness. So altho it should not be eaten in excess, yet one should follow his natural—mark well we say *natural*—taste and eat it when needed. Therefore, those who strive to follow the true teachings of the Christ are truly "the salt of the earth," *i.e.*, are a means of preserving in humanity the unimpeded flow of the Divine Life-force of the Christ.

> "Why is it that if living beings are not merely the result of cellular organization, that certain functions of the body can be kept up for a time after death when removed from the rest of the body? Biologists say that death is merely the disruption of certain cell action, so that the different organs no longer act in unison."
> March 2, 1923.

The conception of modern scientists, who are practically all materialists, that life is merely the product of cellular action, is putting the cart before the horse. As a matter of fact life exists and existed before there was any aggregation of physical cells capable of expressing it. In fact, the cells are aggregated and differentiated by the invisible Ideal of each species for the purpose of producing an organism or instrument through which the life current can find expression here in the physical world. Manifestly then, any aggregation of cells merely forms an avenue for expression of the life-forces and centers of consciousness in the invisible worlds which are ever pressing outward for manifestation in the physical world, just as every pipe, faucet or other form of outlet would give expression to the water stored in a reservoir. It would be folly to say that the water is the product of the faucet or pipe.

The tissues removed from the living body and kept alive in proper solutions are simply such faucets, and the life will continue to flow through them as long as the waste products are not allowed to clog up the channel or poison the protoplasm itself and thus not destroy the life but merely prevent it from manifesting through that avenue. Under these conditions it is not the entity of the animal manifesting, but is the current of universal life-force which keeps them active.

There was a time during the grossest stage of materialism in the past nineteenth century, when life as a Principle, separate from the body through which it manifests, was thought to have been disproved and outgrown, and this conception still lingers among a certain class of material scientists and is set forth in many of our other text books. But that too is being outgrown and we are coming to see, largely thru the discoveries in regard to radium and radiant energy, that life is a Principle and that the atomic changes which the materialists thought produced life were but the changes resulting from the wear and tear, we might say, of life manifesting through them in the physical world.

Therefore do not worry yourself by trying to refute

Health and Disease 21

these lingering doctrines of materialism, but hold fast to the idea that materialism as a source of either lifeforce or mind, has been entirely abandoned by the advanced scientists of the day and is only clung to by what we might call the "little fellows," or followers who depend on authority instead of thinking for themselves.

Another evidence that life exists independent of and separate from the body is the fact that the Society for Psychical Research, especially the investigations of Madame Bisson and Professor Geley of Paris and Dr. von Schrenk Notzing of Munich, in regard to the ectoplasm, etc., and the photographs taken of persons long deceased, prove conclusively and from a materialistic standpoint, *i.e.*, through the camera, that they still live, altho their physical bodies or the instruments which they required to manifest in the physical world, had long since disintegrated in the grave or been cremated. This is an absolute positive proof, and even materialistically proves, that life continues on, independent of the physical body after it has been thrown off or left behind.

> "Every month I find much in the lessons which seems to have been written personally for me. I often lend my lessons to people who have showed interest in such matters. I received almost instant relief the moment I wrote to the Teacher."
> Sept 12, 1922.

We are glad the lessons come to you monthly as a real personal help. This is truly a proof that these Teachings come from a Divine Teacher who knows the wants of all His children; for only one who understood the hearts of many and could look deep into their lives could so answer the questions most pertinent to their conditions. We are also glad to have you lend the lessons to your friends, for you are thus doing much good.

We rejoice that your health is better and that you felt the almost instant relief after having written to the Teacher. This is because the instant you ask in the name of the Order for health or help, the Masters back of the Order hear and answer you. Of course you must write to the Agents, who are but human, to give them an understanding of the thing before getting your answer by letter, but the Divine Teachers hear and answer immediately, altho the answer may not always come just as you expect or think it should. If you will realize this, there may be many times in your life when you need help and yet, thinking of the time it takes for a letter to reach America, many hesitate to ask it. But if you sit down for a few moments and try to realize that this Order is a band of devoted Souls who are trying to put forth the real work of love and help and healing through the Great Teacher who is back of this Order; that it is this Great Teacher who watches over everyone who joins their hands and hearts with this band, then you can ask and know that because you are helping and have joined His chosen band of disciples, you are sure to be heard and sure to be helped according to what He knows is best to manifest to you.

Chapter II

PSYCHIC CONDITIONS

> "A woman on the next ranch used to go into trances, not because she wanted to, but because she could not stop herself. I have seen as many as eight or ten personalities have possession of her. From the time that I heard that she died a terror came over me. I would feel a terrible cold feeling in my forehead, then a chilly sensation up my spine and a terrible drawing at the base of the brain. I wrote to the school and they told me to bathe my head in salt water, eat raw meat ground with onions and to eat vegetables grown under ground."
>
> April 14, 1923.

As to what you say about having seen eight or ten personalities in possession of the medium, this is particularly important for you to understand, because we must never permit ourselves to be obsessed by any person either seen or unseen; either a so-called spirit entity or an earthly personality. One of the greatest lessons we have to learn in this life is to express our own selves.

If you will read our book, *Realms of the Living Dead*, you will see that there is a higher form of spiritualism by which the higher spiritual entities can instruct us, but without taking possession of us. In the early stages of psychism we must use all our power and force to see that no one takes possession of us. All the messages we receive from such undeveloped spirits—as the mediums are in the habit of calling them—are simply from undeveloped mortals who have passed on and know little more than when on earth. If they had good judgment while on earth their judgment is still good, but if they were ignorant while here then they are almost as ignorant now as they were then. Hence we have no reason to think what they are telling us is wisdom, altho their intentions may be good.

The terror you felt after your friend passed out showed plainly that she was doing her best, altho ignorantly, to get possession of you and was bringing those sensations, not through her will, but simply because she in turn was obsessed by other astral entities far lower than herself and with more vicious tendencies. You should not take teachings from this woman now any more than you would were she on earth. No matter how good she may have been, she had certainly not evolved high enough to give you any true teaching.

We have quite a different way of helping our pupils than that of the school you mention. We say you should demand, "In the Name of the living Christ," that the astral entities be kept from you.

It is not that you are to keep up the fight, but that you are to stop fighting and rely entirely on Divine Help. You must never fight or hope to have victory over these obsessing entities, but simply call upon the Christ and think of yourself as surrounded by the aura or the great Light of the Christ, who always comes to you when you call, and you will be protected. That which to you is but a protecting wall of beautiful radiant Christ-light is to those obsessing entities a burning fire which they dare not enter; consequently they leave you at once. This is the only way to close the door. Alas, you did have your astral doors open, as have so many persons who have not had the right teaching. The only way to close them is to ask the living Christ to come and stand in the doorway, and then His power, not yours, His love and His force will make such a great stream of intensified fiery force that nothing which can harm you will come near you.

All the things the . . . . school told you are absolutely useless, because they are only on the outer physical plane. You must first correlate with the Christ in your heart and in your mind and learn to love Him because He is your protector and will always come at your call.

It is no wonder that the . . . . society itself so soon fell under the spell of astral obsession, and its leader was disgraced and ruined, if this is a sample of the teachings they gave to the Souls who came to them earnestly seeking for Truth. No doubt it was all they could do to help you; and no doubt they thought they were helping you, but you must have proved its utter fallacy. So we say put away all these childish things and determine that henceforth you will rest your cause with the Lord Christ.

> "Under the advice of a psychic friend I tried certain experiences on retiring, supposedly to effect contact with the astral. Later I heard ominous rumblings, a pandemonium of voices, and experienced fearsome sinking sensations. The room seemed peopled, yet I saw nothing."
> Sept 12, 1922.

If you read and study our book, *Realms of the Living Dead*, you will find that we do not believe in encouraging our pupils to go through any exercises which will open them to the astral. We also explain thoroughly the danger of such practices and how unwise it is for a beginner to undertake any such experiences. Therefore, if you are going to study with us, we advise you to stop at once all such exercises and to follow our Teachings on the subject.

Evidently you are rushing ahead like an engine

without an engineer and your course is quite as dangerous as would be that of the engine.

We do not condemn what you have received, and some of it may have come from the right source. But you must know and you must challenge. It is far better to go slowly and to receive instruction from one whom you know than to gain a great deal of heterogeneous information from you know not whom or where.

Certainly you are not only eligible, but you need our instruction very much; for when a person begins to get psychic phenomena he does need the hand of a Teacher—such a one as is back of this movement and who dictates the letters—to guide him, lest the engine without the driver should run off the track.

> "A form appeared to me with a cloak and turban on and called to me. It felt like something opposing me."
>
> April 14, 1923.

Whenever anyone comes to you, even tho he comes in what looks to be the form of the Christ, or if he comes in a cloak and turban and claims to be some great Teacher, always say, "In the name of the living Christ, I challenge you. If you are a servant of the Christ, prove it to me by standing on my right hand. If you cannot, begone and never come near me again." If this challenge is said from the depths of your heart, it is always answered. And if that which comes is for your good, the radiant light which comes from such a person will stream out with greater abundance, and the love-light in the eyes will assure you of its genuineness. If it is false, it will disappear. Do this whenever you see beings approach you, or in dreams or in psychic experiences. Those who love you, the servants of the King of Kings, delight in obedience to the challenge and they expect pupils to use it. Those who are false, however, may do all in their power to convince you that it is foolish and that of course you know them to be all right, etc. But be warned, for this is most important.

> "About ten years ago, after sensing the warm vibrant life in my arms and legs I sensed it in my sacral plexus. I tasted heaven for two weeks, then I awoke and found myself back in the old state of consciousness. Shortly after this I had a vision of a large Oriental room and heard many voices."
> March 10, 1923.

Your experience was but a temporary opening of the veil during which you caught a glimpse of the possibilities awaiting you if you follow diligently the tasks which are set before you. But only too often under such circumstances students are so carried away by the apparent change in all their surroundings that they think they are done with trials and troubles and that they will forever after live in peace and harmony; hence they cease to strive or to look out for the temptations which come to them, and consequently they fall back. We must realize that every experience of this kind is merely to show us that to which we can attain, not to what we have already attained. Unless we go on working even harder because of the possibilities we see ahead of us, we are apt to spend our time in congratulating ourselves, and perhaps in saying to our friends that we have reached a place of perfect harmony; or that we have passed a great initiation, etc.

When we do this we are sure to find, ere we realize it, that we are back in our old state of consciousness, and because of the experience we have had we feel it much worse and more difficult to conquer, and we are apt to lose our faith in the Divine Love and guidance, and to say, "What is the use?"

All these experiences which you feel in your hands, etc., should not be noticed, for when we are developing the Christ-consciousness in us, we are told to "kill out sensation." This does not mean to kill out the ordinary sensations of earthly life but to kill out all sensations which come not as a part of our spiritual realization of oneness but as the astral effort to make us satisfied with sensation instead of manifesting the reality.

> "When you see things and places which you have never visited to get the impression and see accidents to others, and work perhaps in places of which you know nothing, have never seen or even read of, the inside of buildings you have never entered, does this come from the sub-conscious mind?"
>
> June 15, 1923.

Pre-vision and clairvoyance or that which the psychologists wrongly ascribe to the subconscious mind, is the power to catch glimpses of distant things and places which you may or may not have experienced either in this or in past lives.

However, that which you describe as your experience is not such a memory. These experiences are the wanderings of your ethereal or astral body, and its astral consciousness, through certain scenes and places, most of them right here on this physical earth; scenes and places it is attracted to either through affinity or perhaps because at some time you are to come into touch with them; or they may have to do with persons with whom you are acquainted, or possibly may come out of past lives.

This is a very common experience, for altho when we go to sleep this inner ethereal astral body is released, and altho it has the possibility of going up into the higher realms, it usually, unless directed by us to do otherwise, is apt to remain in what we call the astral counterpart of this world and passes through all kinds of experiences; enters, as you say, into buildings of whose interior you never had any consciousness; and meets with other experiences, all of which, however, are in some way destined to come to you or to those with whom you are associated.

Yet it is not wise to permit this, for it disturbs your rest and you are almost as tired out when you awaken as tho you had been taking these wanderings when in your physical body. For this reason we advise our pupils to say some prayer before dropping to sleep (our *Prayer for Protection* is a good one for this) and make a stronger effort to ascend into the higher realms where they may have complete rest, peace and harmony and leave the world with all its troubles and all its experiences behind them.

The subconscious mind is merely the consciousness of the organs and functions of the body synthesized into the animal soul. Its business is to take care of these functions, *i.e.*, digestion, circulation, respiration, etc., and in fact to see to the proper functioning of all the organs of the body.

> "I am soon to be married. . . .
> "Last year when sleeping alone I experienced sensual uncanny chills right through the body. Are these astral chills and, if so, how can they be remedied?"

We congratulate you not only upon your coming marriage but also upon the way you contemplate it, as a sacred and holy thing. We are glad that you feel you have had the guidance which assures you that this is the right and proper marriage for you to make.

As to the chills you speak of, such uncanny chills

mean that something unpleasant or sensual from the astral plane is near you, and if it is disturbing you you should order it away. Such a chill must not be allowed to continue, so we advise that you say very positively, "In the name of the living Christ, begone." Do not fear it, for there is nothing to be afraid of, because such entities must obey the force of the Christ which you invoke. We are told in the *Bible* that at the name of Jesus, *i.e.*, Jesus the Christ, every knee shall bow and every tongue shall confess His supremacy. Also in the astral world, which is just a little above the physical world, absolute obedience is given to this name. The only time when such entities will not leave you after you make such a positive demand in the name of the Christ is when you have a half-conscious desire to know something about them; then the demand is not truly positive as it should be, for you have left an open door.

Of course there is always something in our character which permits such contacts, for until we reach complete Mastery we can never say there is nothing in our aura that is wrong. But the question is not that we shall never go wrong but that we shall still believe and hope and trust in our Lord Jesus Christ and know that whatever is wrong shall be righted if we but keep on trying, keep on praying, keep on relying upon His help and guidance.

> "My husband has the drink habit, not all the time but periodically, the periods becoming more frequent. How do you explain this?"
> Aug. 11, 1923.

As a general thing this comes from something that is more or less of an obsession. Nine-tenths of those addicted to the drinking habit, owing to the effect of alcohol on the psychic centers, are more or less open to the astral world and to persons in the astral who have passed over because of drink, or who have spent their earth life in drinking and still desire to have the sensation of drink through more or less sensitive people on the physical plane. This can be obtained vicariously through another by obsessing or throwing the desire over him and causing him to drink.

There is but one way to treat this. The victim must demand "In the Name of the Living Christ" that all entities shall keep away from him so that they cannot obsess him or give him the desire for drink. If you can explain this to your husband and get his co-operation in it, it would be well. For very often this fact awakens in one the manly idea that he will not suffer for the sake of giving someone else such satisfaction or relief, and he will therefore refuse to drink when the feeling comes over him.

The reason it seems to come a little oftener now than previously is because there is such a great fight to maintain this old idea that a person has a right to drink if he wants to. If it is possible to replace this with a "Thou shalt," namely, "Thou shalt strive for higher things and not permit obsessing entities to force you to do something your Higher Self does not approve of,"—if this can be impressed upon him, he will cure himself. Do not worry over it; do not comment upon it. Do not blame him; that is, do not blame him for what he does, but try to help him to strengthen his forces against the entitized powers that are striving to make him a mere tool to satisfy their appetites.

> "I am glad to say that through your help I am free again from the power of drink. I am again a happy man, and my family also."
> Aug. 17, 1922.

We are rejoiced to hear that through following our Teachings you have broken away from the demon drink. You can always depend upon our prayers and help, but remember that no one else can cure you; it must be by your own constant and determined effort. To keep yourself free from drink try to realize to its fullest extent that you yourself are powerful and do not want to drink; that the craving is an obsession by some outside entity trying to make use of you to satisfy his lower appetites.

Try to awaken in yourself this knowledge and keep on saying to yourself: "I do not want it. I will not have it. No one shall make me take it." Then fill yourself with the love of the Christ and keep on affirming that this love and this power and this help will keep you free from any evil influence.

Dear brother, do not think that the victory is absolutely won until you have let the thought of the loving Christ and the desire of your own Divine Self enter in and take the place of the excitement which was formerly supplied by the drink. Fill yourself so full of this thought of the Christ that no outside entity can come and tempt you.

> "Will you kindly tell me if there is any truth whatever in so-called spiritualism, and can you recommend any medium in San Francisco who is reliable and true?"
>
> July 2, 1923.

Let us say, first, that we thoroughly investigated all the phenomena of spiritualism many years ago and proved it absolutely authentic in many cases, hence have given little attention to it in subsequent years, as that is not our work. We are not personally familiar with the mediums in San Francisco who could give you trustworthy demonstrations.

As to our own work, the proven facts of spiritualism are but the kindergarten steps, in fact but the A B C. For our work, although spiritual, is far more than spiritualism, inasmuch as it gives the fundamental and cosmic laws of Divine Manifestation in all the worlds, together with the spiritual principles underlying all great religions. It also explains the methods of interpreting the allegorical and symbolic accounts to be found in all scriptures. We are enclosing a letter and pamphlet which describes our method of work and our Teachings. They are simply placed before you and you take from them as much as you are ready for or able to take, and let the rest remain until it appeals to you.

Although our *Realms of the Living Dead* does not present the evidential side of spiritualism—as that can be found in many, many other volumes—it does give you a synthetic view of the whole subject, scientifically differentiated so that you can understand the sources of the many classes of phenomena and can reconcile the many discrepancies which seem to occur in the phenomena of Spiritualism.

> "To my mind it seems like an intrusion to bring back those of our loved ones who have passed over, and to show them in pictures to audiences. Yet I feel assured of his sincerity and earnestness."
> Aug. 2, 1923.

We are glad the remarks about . . . .awoke in your heart an understanding of not so much our belief in the sincerity and earnestness of the work he and his dear wife are doing, but of one of the fundamental teachings of this Order, which is, that we must express brotherhood and kindliness and consideration toward all who are sincerely and earnestly striving to bring help to humanity in their best understanding of how that help can be given, even if they differ somewhat from us.

As far as as . . . .'s work is concerned, we personally feel very much as you do about it. But the

Founders know, especially from their close and intimate connection with the . . . ., that there are hundreds and thousands of people in this world who are not capable of making the touch with their beloved ones in the heart or of feeling the overshadowing of Divine Consciousness. And these must have absolutely physical demonstration ere they can believe. Now, if these pictures and the Teachings of . . . .can awaken even a small number of this particular class of people and start them on the way to study the real philosophy, then they have done a great deal of good. We believe this will be the result of his work.

As to it being an intrusion to commune with those who have passed on, we must remember that we should intrude neither on those who have passed out or on our friends here on earth. But there are many who are very eager to help us and who are waiting for recognition, and such recognition is an avenue for communion with those who are eagerly waiting for just such an opportunity. However, this is not the work of this Order any more than is that of the Salvation Army, altho we give to both our sincere sympathy and brotherly understanding, for we know there are many whom we could never touch but whom they can help, and vice versa. Therefore, God bless them all.

Chapter III

KARMA

"How can I recognize my Karma and work for the Order?"

July 6, 1923.

The great law of Karma or cause and effect places every personality in just the place and condition in life which will naturally bring it into touch with the lesson that is needed. However, every little thing that comes to you is not karmic, but is a part of the kind of conditions you must learn to overcome. For instance, if in your life you have to mingle with people who irritate you and tend to awaken in you unkind thoughts, etc., it simply means that your Karma is to overcome such thoughts and actions and to demonstrate over those conditions. If you are placed in poverty, it means perhaps that you are there to learn how to recognize the fact that you do not have to be poor; that if you love your Father-in-Heaven and obey Him He will take care of you and bring to you all that you need, if you do your part. So we might go on describing special conditions, but remember that Karma is not the Karma of every little event, but that Karma simply guides you into conditions where you will meet with the lessons you need and where you may learn the higher lessons you must learn. Karma is an urge to awaken you to your higher divine possibilities, very much as a father might put a wayward, thoughtless son into some position where the hard work and difficulties he would meet would make a man of him. Therefore, your work for the Order will unfold as you are ready for it.

> "Is it best to call down all your past Karma, so that you can wipe it out in one life?"
> April 11, 1922.

It is a great mistake to demand that we shall have all our Karma given to us in one life. It is just as great a misunderstanding of the Divine Law and just as wrong as to try to eat at one meal all the food needed for a week. The great angelic Lords of Karma apportion to each Soul *exactly what each Soul is able to bear* and work out *advantageously* in each life. Yet the Law is that if we demand and insist we must be allowed to have our demand, and by the sad experiencing of that for which we are not prepared or able to use learn our lessons just as we would learn through indigestion not to eat all the food in sight. But we need not have gone through the suffering had we been willing to accept what the Law had apportioned to us.

If we ask for all our Karma to be precipitated the great load is poured out upon us before we are strong enough to cope with it and we are forced to admit our weakness and turn to the Great Law for help; for we have tried to do in one life that which should have been spread out over many lives as we were ready to work it out constructively and harmoniously. Moreover, by making the demand we have made more Karma.

In a sense, such a demand is an impertinent and conceited rebuke to the great Lords of Karma, for it assumes that Their judgment as to what is best for us is inferior to our own. Also if our entire time and attention is taken up in fighting and being pushed to the utmost to bear that which was not assigned to us, we have little time and strength left to cultivate the positive qualities of love and joy or to help others. Yet in this world of sorrow and trouble it is most important that these qualities be definitely cultivated and lifted up and radiated, especially by those who are at all advanced and to whom others may look for help and guidance and example, and thus make the world a little less like a purgatory. Therefore we make a great mistake when we try so to fill our lives with negative Karma to be redeemed that we make our lives joyless.

You will thus see that very often when we think ourselves the least selfish we are in reality manifesting but a higher sort of selfishness and a sort of personal pride in the amount of suffering we are able to bear. If you do not care for worldly things and it is no deprivation to do without them—hence it is no sacrifice—yet all the time you are ardently desiring other possessions, personal powers, etc., can you not see that when we demand the thing we desire most we are asking for the gratification of our own wishes just as much as if they were for material possessions, while we should be joyously and happily taking what our Father sees is best and asking daily for strength and wisdom to utilize it wisely and learn its lessons? When we strive to make the Divine Will our will we have strength to meet and conquer all things and are never overwhelmed.

We tell you plainly that you cannot expect supernatural help to bear burdens which the Great Law never intended you should bear in one life. We have many important things to learn and do in life besides bearing burdens and suffering. And sometimes it is more difficult to turn our minds away from ourselves and our woes and be joyful and radiate happiness than it is to crucify ourselves; for we have to be very far advanced indeed to hang upon the cross and still radiate joy to the world instead of suffering and agony.

> "Since all that comes to me is but a reflection of something in myself, how can I avoid my fate? And am I responsible for what I do, since all is but an illusion?"

Aug. 15, 1923.

You certainly have not received the teaching from us which tells you that everything that happens to you or comes to you is but a reflection of something in yourself. What we do say is that there is a certain Karma—taking Karma to mean cause and effect—which in past incarnations you have set up and built into your character, and this naturally brings you in touch with certain conditions. And because they are the result of such cause and effect, these conditions are very difficult to meet and conquer. For the cause of them is built into your nature, hence you should understand the true meaning of Karma; that it is not only the cause of these conditions built into you, but also an opportunity to gain the power to overcome their effects.

Therefore it is very different from that which we call fate. For instance, suppose you had as Karma inherited a bad temper and the effect of this temper would naturally be to bring you into many difficult conditions. Yet in the very inheritance of this temper there is the power to overcome the difficulty. For instance, Karma has brought you into touch with this Order and its higher Teachings and thus you are taught to know how to work to overcome whatever difficulties you meet with. It may be other things besides temper; it may be the inability to earn a living or some other factor. We have merely used the instance of bad temper as an illustration. But this is the meaning of everything that comes to you being within yourself. The lack of certain qualities within you brings to you certain conditions until those lacking qualities are developed, hence there is more or less difficulty in seeing the other side. Yet there is always within you a way out of the difficulties, if you ask by the power of the Christ to find it.

As we permit our consciousness to dwell amid the confusion of world-thought, these world-thoughts seek to overpower our own individual thoughts of oneness with the Divine. There are two things we give you for concentration and we ask you to try your best to fix your thoughts upon them. First, say to yourself, "I am a child of God, one with my Father. My Divine Mother is Love. My Divine Life is the Christ. I am one with all this and I can and must draw my thought-force from this source." The second is: "Since I am a child of the Godhead, I have come into this physical world to work out certain things both in myself and in the world. I can only do this by my realization of my oneness with my Father-Mother, and also my oneness with all my brothers and sisters in the world."

Remember our Soul, the Divine part of us, is one with God. Our personality and our physical conditions in the world are one with all mankind. We are not here for our own salvation wholly, but equally to uplift and bless and help all humanity. Therefore take the two ideas we have given you for your month's work. For a long time if necessary you may repeat them just as words, but never fail to do it. Repeat them three times a day at least and as often as you feel the call to do so in the course of the day. But later on you will find that you do not have to repeat them as words, for something of their true meaning has sunk into your heart. And when this occurs, strive to live them instead of saying them.

> "Since your last letter I have been going through the shock and change that come with the death of a dear loved one. The death-bed scene was terrible and in a war a test of my belief and faith. The question with me through the long period of her great suffering was. Why should she who was of a gentle and unselfish nature, have to undergo such long drawn-out suffering? She would not let go physical life until death had beaten her into a corner."
>
> Sept. 16, 1922.

There are many gentle, beautiful Souls who have been brought up with the idea that death is terrible and that we must hold on to the physical body until the last possible moment. Such Souls do bring to themselves much unnecessary suffering, especially if the creed of punishment, etc., has been imbued into them.

Another reason is of course karmic. Many Souls today who are spiritually advanced have nevertheless in the past lived the life of renunciation and have taught humanity the necessity for suffering and punishment until they have really built it into their own lives. And consequently only as they come back and live a life in which they literally pass through the experiences they have taught themselves and others to believe are necessary, can they truly be ready, after this life of suffering is over, to realize that they had made a great mistake.

As you doubtless know, what we call the higher plane is, for those who are ready to receive it, all that we can contemplate of heaven and joy, etc., while the world in which we suffer and pay our karmic debts is Hell—all the hell there is. When we say this we do not mean it as a positive or enduring assertion, but we mean it as especially applying to the past dark ages. In other words, there are planes and planes and there is an especial place which is called heaven by many. And this place has been literally created during what the world calls the dark ages, by the church which has taught these doctrines of an atonement to be attained only through mortification of the flesh, etc. This is also one meaning of Jesus descending into hell to help the spirits imprisoned there. Therefore those who have earnestly striven with all their hearts to live up to the ideals of the church often find themselves confined to such a place after death. It is a heaven in one sense, but in it they find only the realization of the ideals held out to them: for instance, a crucified and a risen Savior; a heart-searching of all their faults and a literal judgment.

Such persons must incarnate again upon Earth and they incarnate with all the beauties of their devotion, all the lessons they have gathered, all the desires for a higher and better life; but they have not as yet learned the true lessons of life. They often pass thru the karmic result, not only of their sins as do others who have been more worldly, but the results of their beliefs. And because they think this Earth is the only place where they can really atone, they cling to it and pass through much suffering before they let go.

> "What is the attitude of the Order in regard to the binding power of a pledge given to any Order or its heads? How can you explain what is meant by precipitating Karma? Can we precipitate Karma upon another?"
>
> May 1, 1921.

The reason this Order does not demand pledges is because we expect each sincere and earnest student to pledge himself, not to us or to the Order, but to the Christ, and then to keep that pledge to the best of his ability.

As to precipitating Karma, if any human being demands of another a pledge to himself rather than to the Christ, that human being is making for himself a great Karma. Also the one so pledging himself to a mortal is helping that mortal to store up this great Karma which must some time be reaped.

As to the possibility of precipitating Karma upon another, under certain conditions we would say it is possible, but these certain conditions are as follows: If we give a pledge to another and do not keep it, or if we help another person to exalt his personality; if we consciously do anything to place another person in a supreme position which only the highest spiritual Teachers should occupy, we are precipitating Karma upon that person. If any high spiritual Teacher did occupy such a supreme position he would prove his spirituality by his willingness to ask that the pupil should pledge himself only to the Christ and promise to do his best to help on the great work.

We are all instruments of Karma really to help one another, for remember that Karma is not punishment, but is something brought to us in love that we may learn to avoid some mistake and to learn some great lesson, yet we are responsible when we use our own judgment and say, "Such and such a thing is needed by so-and-so and therefore I will do something to teach him his lesson," or help to place a person in a position where his Karma will be precipitated upon him.

Try to realize the difference between a human being deliberately making up his mind that he is going to rebuke another, and being but an unknowing instrument which the Great Law uses to bring a lesson to another. There is a big difference between the two, for as we have said above, every one is in the hands of the Great Law, and much of the Karma which comes to us and to others comes through the instrumentality of some other human being.

> "I seem to be meeting the Karma of two different incarnations, and two Paths are ahead of me. Whichever I choose, I am haunted by the fear that I am failing another Soul. I do not know where the human me should be."

As to meeting the Karma of two different incarnations at the same time and as to two paths being ahead of you, this cannot be explained exactly in this way. For the Karma we meet is the accumulated Karma not of two incarnations but of all our incarnations. In other words, we must meet and conquer all those things which, altho we may meet them again and again, we have so far failed to conquer.

Also when you say there are two paths for you to choose from, apparently intimating that each path belongs to a separate incarnation, you are not fully grasping or understanding the subject. Two paths are always before the eyes of the aspirant for the Divine Wisdom. The one path represents the natural physical path of evolution which you have followed incarnation after incarnation and yet have not fully conquered or understood. It is the result of previous teachings and world ideas which your birth under various conditions has built into your flesh, as it were, or let us say it is the Karma of the personality rather than of the Soul.

The other path is the path which the Soul itself has chosen. There are always steps which we meet when striving to follow these two paths and which we must find out for ourselves. But once we have deliberately chosen to walk in the path of the Divine Light we know we have our guidance and our help; that whatever else comes up it is not a thing to be smothered or killed, but is something that has come to us as a result of our special development. Therefore it is to be blended into the Divine Path which we have chosen; that is, we are to lay it on the altar of the Christ and ask, not that we be given strength to destroy it and discard it, but that we be shown what amount of good there is in it and how we are to use this special idiosyncracy to reach the highest attainment.

No two Souls reach the heights by taking just the same steps. The very fact that there is such a diversity of steps—each in its own place—is evidence that all things are to be laid upon the altar, and be purified and their lessons learned and blended into the spiritual path we have chosen. In other words, we are not to kill out every tendency, but we must discard that part of them which we find holds us back and interferes with our progress to the spiritual heights. We must start with the idea that we are individuals, perhaps quite different from any other individual on the face of the earth, because ruled by special planetary conditions, with certain special tendencies and traits which are still undeveloped and unfinished and crude. These are the goods which have been given to us by our Father when we were sent into this far country of earth-life. And instead of wasting them in riotous living—letting these personalities and traits run away with us—we must take them up one by one and use them for the highest good and ask that the blessing of the Almighty be poured upon them.

> "What I want to know chiefly is, what makes me suffer, and how can I get more peaceful, less irritable and more loving to other people? I have such lots of antagonism in my family. I feel as if I could never get over them. It is for these others I am trembling and nervous. Is this my Karma?"

There is just one way to become more peaceful and to keep the affairs of the family from worrying you: that is, to realize that you are a child of God and that God not only takes care of you, but also of all the

Family; that what comes to the family is their problem and not yours. And if they ask for the solution it will be given them. Your only duty in connection with it is to help them to understand it.

One of the greatest mistakes is to worry about what comes to our family or friends. Remember that nothing comes to them that is our personal business. The way to go on under such circumstances is to realize absolutely—and when we say realize we do not mean merely the saying of it, but the absolute believing—that you are a child of God; that you are in this physical embodiment purposely to learn the lessons most necessary for you; that He is with you and is watching over you. And if you show the right attitude of mind or the true desire to do the right thing, you will not only be helped but will hear the answer plainly, or at the very least will be led into doing that which is right.

Nothing can keep us back that is not our business. Nothing can keep us back from lifting the curtain on our own life, but it is not our business to lift the curtain from anyone else's life. We must do our own work and be cheerful, happy and helpful, but we must not even try to do someone else's work. Suggest, perhaps, what you think is wise and then leave them alone; for each one must take the Karma of what he decides to do. So if we tell others to do something against their will, then, as the old Scotchman says, "They will surely be of the same opinion still."

As to your nervous state, first of all do as we have told you, *i.e.,* mind your own affairs, attune yourself to the God of Love and let all your household and their various duties rest in His great love. Know absolutely that whatever is best for them will come to them and no amount of worry or the disturbance of your own conditions can possibly change it. But pray that they may be enlightened and guided to do and follow that which is best.

> "Words at my command would fail to give due expression to the appreciation I have for the wonderful service you are doing for mankind, myself in particular . . . . Assuming that reincarnation is optional with our Real Selves, why is there such a conformity to peculiarities and weaknesses in several members of the one family?"
>
> Nov. 10, 1922.

As to "assuming that reincarnation is optional with our Real Selves," this not so in all cases. Our real Divine Self is sent down by the great Lord of Life to clothe itself in matter again and again until, first, it can lift up and spiritualize that matter which composes its own physical body and as this is completed, help to spiritualize and uplift the matter of the whole world. Therefore this is not optional.

Our own higher Divine Self—being a part of God in the same way that the sunlight which shines into our windows is surely one with and a part of the Sun in the heavens—earnestly desires above all things to help the great work of informing, spiritualizing and uplifting the matter of this globe. In our own Divine Self we do not differentiate between that particular part of matter which we call our own personality, for we know it is but fleeting, yet we also know that in our personal selves, we often add to the burden of the forces which are holding this world away from the oneness with God. Therefore, in our next incarnation this burden is added to the general task which is ours, and which is willingly assumed, not optionally chosen. This we call Karma.

Remember, there is a great differentiation between Karma and the real purpose of the immortal Soul. As we have said, that purpose is to help in the perfecting of the globe, whereas Karma is seeing our own personal faults, correcting them, and bringing the personal self into oneness with the Divine Self. The physical conditions running through a family are therefore the physical heredity of the parents or the family Karma which the Soul must assume when entering that particular family.

Chapter IV

COMING WORLD CHANGES[1]

> "Much has been given to me by the Voice and in vision about coming catastrophies that I seldom talk about. Is this the right attitude?"
>
> Aug. 2, 1923.

Our teachings on these subjects are that it is not wise to give our students definite particulars of the conditions that are coming. All the Teachings that the Master gives us are given with great love and hope, as they point out unerringly the power of overcoming these conditions. For unregenerate man, and even those of us who have advanced to a certain degree, if we are shown the special disasters, etc., that are coming, are apt to let them prey on our minds, and we forget to hold fast to the hand that guides us and to know that whatever comes, all is well. Or else we are apt to feel that we will be protected while others may suffer; and it is but human then to allow a feeling of superiority to creep into our minds.

At the same time we know there are some persons who should be allowed to see and understand these things, because they need to pass through the lessons these things can teach. Therefore there are certain teachers who do show such things. Yet you must remember there is a vast difference between having these things shown to yourself and being a teacher to whom the lesson given is not for himself but for many Souls who are looking to him for help. So in our work of teaching we are specially impressed with the comfort

---

[1] This subject is now more fully treated in the book *Coming World Changes*, Curtiss.

and hope and love that this great New Age is bringing, even though old things must pass away before all things can be made new.

Know well there is no such thing as punishment; that if anyone is killed in such disasters or any country is wiped out, it is only that they may come back again with greater knowledge and a realization that they must be true and helpful to humanity; that God is Love personified; that this Love rules the world, altho sometimes it is necessary for these seemingly terrible conditions to prevail for a time.

> "Should we allow our knowledge that disasters are coming and inevitable to make us fearful of the future? .... How can we prevent this?"
> Jan. 11, 1923.

We have no fear of any of the disasters which are predestined, yet we know they are coming. Another thing the Teacher has told us is that the closer we all stand together the better we will be able to send our influence to help those who are endangered. This is the prediction of the great cleaning up of the fields of mankind or the garnering in of the harvest. Before the golden grains can be readily garnered, the chaff must be winnowed and burned.

Therefore stand firm. Have no fear, and come as close to us in heart and mind as you can. We know there are great things coming and that it is necessary for us all to be true and loving and devoted; to forget ourselves in the help and uplift we are sending out to the world. We have no doubt but that America will have to take her share as well as the other countries in the world, but we cannot imagine that America will suffer as much. Firstly, she is larger and can spread out more; secondly, she is younger and has not made quite so much bad Karma; thirdly, we firmly believe this is the country in which is to be established the Great Temple in which the true Wisdom Religion shall spread to the world. But it needs all of us to help to spread it. We must forget self and work together for the Masters and the good of all humanity.

> "I have made six copies of the *Prayer for World Harmony,* my copy having gone to the Pacific Coast and back again and is now in New York . . . . Why should we have to pass through the conditions indicated?"
>
> Oct 12, 1922.

We know well that humanity is liable to continue to pass through some of the most terrible conditions it has ever yet known. This is the breaking up and the working out of the Karma of the old sub-race and the preparation for the new. The new and greater day cannot be ushered in without this clearing up of the Karma of the old conditions. In the terrible days coming we must not grow cold or distant, but must stand very, very close together, for only so can we send out enough thought-force of love and purity and helpfulness practically to redeem the world. At present, so many are giving way to thoughts of violence and inharmony that there must be a large enough band of those who can think vital loving thoughts, to stand close together, and close to the Christ, and to send out enough love and peace to counteract the evil and to build the foundation for the New Day. For verily if such a band can hold together the Voice of the Lord Christ will be heard in their midst saying, "Lo, I am here, in the midst of you."

That is the reason we sent out the prayer for better world conditions. The best way for all of us to stand together is to repeat this *Prayer for World Harmony*[2] daily; to spend much of our time in meditating on the

---

[2] See Appendix.

bettering of these conditions. We must not fear the disasters we read of in the papers, nor the troubles which are coming (for there will be many, both political and also physical, such as storms, earthquakes, etc.), but we should fearlessly say, "I will be one of those who will stand fast and will pour out the love of my heart and the understanding of my life to make a nucleus of living force which will redeem and counteract the evil." And when we remember that good is ultimately so much more powerful than evil, we need not despair. One drop of ink will discolor an entire glass of pure water, yet the pure water, if separated from the ink, will bring a life-giving power and force to everything it touches, for it is so much greater than the small thing which seemed to contaminate it.

> "For some days I had a premonition of a change, and sure enough, two days ago came the news that I had been selected for transfer to the Pacific Coast. I wonder if the Unseen Forces are at work, for there seemed to be no cause for the change and it has astonished everybody."
>
> May 10, 1923.

Although this change of which your letter tells us seemed to come out of the blue, nevertheless it was pre-arranged and decided upon in the higher realms. As you no doubt know, there are certain forces watching over and guarding all those who are striving to do the Master's work, especially if such persons happen to be in a line of endeavor in which they can truly be a help to humanity. They are placed just as you were, almost miraculously, in a position where their force can be used when the time comes. Already the ones for each special line of work are being selected and watched and tested, so that there will be no chance of any mistake when the time for action comes.

Now, it is a fact that the world is passing through

such a condition that . . . .may come into action and be called upon to do some very decisive and necessary work, and it is most important that there should be some one in touch with the great Masters of Wisdom; some one who could have much to do with the decisions which must be made and with the work which must be done. Indeed, it is useless for America to think it is going to pass through the coming trials without being touched by them. America being the great country it is, with its great opportunities and its great responsibilities, must pass through crucial tests, because, dear student, all these things coming to the world are not coming as punishment but as tests of character, of nationality and of that which has been put into the country.

When America is drawn into the great vortex of purification and regeneration, every man who has any marked influence in the matter will be put to the greatest tests of character. When this time comes, for which we feel sure you are being prepared in a measure, remember you are not being tested, tried and punished for your own sake; remember that you stand for America and that America has the opportunity, if she will awaken to it, of standing as mistress of the world. But if she fails she must go down and let chaos reign. Therefore we are quite sure that altho this post . . . .seems to have come to you in an unlooked-for and almost amazing manner, nevertheless there is back of it some great purpose; some great purpose in the unfolding of your own character and also some great purpose in the testing of your country.

Never say that your post seems to be of little moment or that what you say or do is not listened to, for you have been purposely chosen and placed there, not by any one Teacher from the other side, but by the great Hierarchy of Watchers who are specially appointed to see to it that this great country of ours has her opportunity to take the leading role among the nations, and to take it with the right spirit.

You know this is a mighty work and a mighty decision, and if we were to look at it simply with the eyes that can see but the personal and mundane happenings of life, it would seem impossible. But if we have the open vision and are in touch with the forces which are working for humanity and the world and preparing for the great changes which are coming about, then we see how each little personality who shows any of the required qualities is picked out and put into a place of trust where just those little possibilities in his character may be made to tell.

And yet, dear student, remember that after all it is you yourself who must meet the situation and live up to the possibilities which are coming. Hold fast to all those beautiful ideals which have seemed to come to you almost unheralded, yet which are in reality but the proof that you are in touch with the Great Ones who are preparing you for the work you are to do. And know absolutely that you will be sustained, guided and helped and taught. Do not expect all of a sudden to see the whole ideal worked out; it will and must be one step at a time. So keep your faith constant and true and your life,—not only for your country, for your duty and for your family, but also for all humanity,—burning like a beacon fire forever brighter and brighter. Never let it fail, for great tests are coming.

> "The atmosphere here (in Europe) is very unrestful. One is in an aura of hate, revenge and immorality that is difficult to counteract and doubly difficult to live in. All standards, spiritual and moral, are trailed in the dust . . . . as regards honesty, morality or the common decencies of life, the irresponsibility, the indiffer-

ence to the welfare of others, the selfishness, the greed, in fact, all the lower propensities are in evidence and have to all appearances completely overwhelmed the truer and brighter qualities of humanity."

March 9, 1923.

Your expression of the conditions in certain parts of Europe is very sad, yet very true. If you have read our books carefully, especially *The Message of Aquaria*, you will find that just these conditions through which the whole world is passing have been predicted by us. It is the most crucial stage through which humanity has as yet passed, altho at the end of every sub-race there is something very similar, and frequently the sinking of certain parts of the world marks the ending of each sub-race.

At present the same dire fate overhangs us all, yet we are told that we can prevent it if the world will co-operate in harmony and brotherliness; also that every human atom who will deliberately strive for harmony and peace can help on this great work. Moreover, man has reached such a point of, let us call it, reconstructive energy that it is possible that the parts destroyed may be reconstructed better than before, and will support a population which has learned a great lesson.

Again, as all peoples send help and try to aid the afflicted ones, the lesson of brotherliness and oneness is learned. However, if humanity does not try to work in harmony and brotherliness, there will have to be a great cataclysmic change in the world's geography, also many wars and the worst conditions we have as yet known. However, we are trying to awaken optimism in our students and also to spread this optimism as much as possible and to proclaim to all the world the possibility of averting all this, or of bringing good out of the evil.

"I have lost all my fortune in the Russian revolution and now I am in a very difficult moment. I feel interiorly an energetic urge to make a more fruitful work, to better arrange my life, to put away the things that are an obstacle to the manifestation of my Real Self. I am praying with great earnestness, and during the prayer I feel within me so great a cry for the liberation of my interior self, and now I feel myself answered, and with your Teachings I feel like coming into a new life and I must help the world."

Dec 18, 1922.

The great lesson for each individual Soul to learn at the present time is absolute tolerance, co-operation and world-wide brotherhood. Each Soul who grasps these ideas and tries to put them into effect is helping not only himself but the whole world. This you will see explained in the ***Prayer for World Harmony***.

However, as we have said, altho there are always certain conditions which are world-wide and belong to all the children of this planet, nevertheless we must have in some way made them our own, else we would not be made to suffer from them. So in seeking within yourself for the personal faults and failings begin by seeking for these general things. Ask yourself, "Am I truly expressing universal brotherhood, tolerance and love? Am I seeking in my heart to cooperate with all? Am I recognizing that all the world is one great family; that if we try to separate ourselves into exclusive nations and sections, etc., we are like brothers and sisters who are continually quarrelling; that our Father and our Divine Mother cannot bring peace and harmony into this great household until the children in it have learned to be brotherly and kindly to one another." Then take up the other faults within yourself. But just at the present time the mighty, vital question of the age is that we shall learn to work together and by so doing save the world from the great disasters which are so quickly coming upon us if we do not listen and obey the plain teachings our Father and our Mother are giving us.

We see from the way you sum up your condition that the idea we are trying to tell you has already been given to you from the inner planes and that it is beginning to come through. Therefore, dear sister, hold fast to it. Repeat it again and again to your own consciousness. Try to live it and to spread it in the world. And altho we may not realize it, yet at this particular time there is a greater possibility of helping the world than ever before since the world began.

The world has reached such a state of unbrotherliness and disruption that unless enough of us wake up to this thought, it will have many terrific disasters. And the Great Teacher, the Christ so soon to come, cannot come until this great housecleaning has taken place, and His own, *i.e.*, those who recognize what is needed and who work with all their hearts to bring it about, have truly joined in heart and have put their shoulders to the wheel; have forgotten all racial and national antagonisms and have sought with all their hearts to bring the Christ-spirit to manifest in the world. The conditions in the world today are much like those mentioned in the *Bible* when Sodom and Gomorrah were to be destroyed: "Peradventure ten shall be found there." And He said, "I will not destroy it for ten's sake."

> "I do appreciate your beautiful *Prayer for World Harmony.* . . . We shall draw attention to your works, and with your kind permission will reproduce in our magazine the *Prayer*, which is so beautiful."
>
> Nov. 20, 1922.

We are especially pleased to see that you have thus emphasized the note of harmony and co-operation, both among individuals and organizations, and have given such a practical demonstration of its working among organizations which might well have taken a selfish attitude of independence and isolation.

It is just this principle of co-operation and brotherhood that must be spread broadcast among mankind if western civilization is to be saved from a lapse into barbarism or worse. For it has been revealed to us that unless this principle can be put into operation, among both classes and nations, Europe will soon see another universal maelstrom of war in which the horrors and miseries of the late Great War will be repeated on an even more far-reaching scale.

Because of this impending catastrophe we were directed to issue our *Prayer for World Harmony* in September, which we feel had much to do with the peaceful adjustment of the English-Turkish crisis at that time, and which we feel will help bring about further adjustments between classes, peoples and governments IF IT CAN BE SUFFICIENTLY WIDELY SPREAD before the world. We are therefore taking the liberty of sending you several copies with the request that you follow your inner guidance in placing them in the hands of those thinkers, students and leaders of thought and government who will have the most influence in spreading its message; for by so doing you will be accomplishing an important part of the work for the Masters and humanity which we are not in a position to accomplish.

Chapter V

CONCERNING THE O. C. M.

> "I asked for more Light (regarding the Order) and I tell you exactly what has come: The Order is an immense Movement, only a small portion of which has filtered through. It belongs to the Builders of the Universe.... It has splendid Beings behind it who are preparing the world for the New Cycle.... It is in touch with the Wisdom Sphere and is spreading the white Light of Truth."
>
> June 9, 1922.

You have a very complete and beautiful idea of this Order, and we are glad to find that you received it from the higher spheres.

As you probably know, the main point in this Order is to give forth Teachings which in no way bind or hold the Soul of any being. In this Order there are no vows made to any earthly body or person. Each Soul who feels the urge to work with and for the Order vows to his own Divine Self, because he believes that this avenue is an avenue of helpfulness to the world. But each Soul is also left absolutely free to follow his own inner guidance. In fact, this is exactly the work which is needed, namely, using discretionary powers to give forth the Truth without limitation or dogmatism to each Soul according to the Soul's capacity to receive it.

We will therefore be glad to have you work with us and for us according to the dictates of your own inner Divine Consciousness. We feel that you could not have had the comprehension of the Order or have received from the higher Beings its exact work, had you not been chosen as one of the workers to bring about, not any success for this Order as an Order under any certain name, but the success of the Great Work destined by the Masters to be given to humanity, namely, the enlightenment of humanity, with absolute freedom from all sectarianism and binding conditions, and the necessity for each Soul to give its vows only to the Divine; and for this reason prove more true than could be done were the vows given to any other mortal. In other words, there is no mortal who stands between the advanced Souls of this Order and their work. There is no one who is willing to take the Karma of such fidelity. We literally throw open the door, but only those who have been tested and are trying to follow the guidance which is given them can hold hands, as it were, with all the other workers and co-operate in the great and marvelous work of this New Day.

By identifying yourself with anything which has so broad and wonderful a mission, could you in any way lose your own work in it? Ask your own Soul: As the Builders of the Universe gather the materials to reinstate the great Wisdom Religion once delivered to humanity, do They not need the work of every devoted Soul? Can any devoted loving labor be lost? Can any identification with co-workers in this great work in any way belittle or diminish the work that another Soul is given to do? In a great Temple are not painters, plasterers, artists, all classes needed to complete the work? and do any of them lose themselves in striving to perfect their part of the work? or do they but enhance it and make it more complete? How much more then, when we are rebuilding the world, do we not need all kinds of laborers?

This Order is preparing the world for a new cycle,

at the present time opening the door of this new cycle, and we need many co-workers, for the work is strenuous. The fields of the world are white with the harvest, but the laborers, or those who can understand and work only for the King of Kings and follow only His commands, are indeed few. Therefore, if your own Soul is to be given the exact meaning of this inner counsel, we are sure you will grasp the fact that in such a great work as preparing the world for a new cycle and spreading to all classes a restatement of the world-old Wisdom Religion, it is very necessary that each one shall stick to his own part of the work, yet that there can be no "Mine and Thine," but only a united co-operation and a fidelity to principles. For without this co-operation and obedience to the Great Architect who is giving out the work, without this fidelity to the plans, there can be nothing, or at least very little, accomplished.

> "I would like to know in what relation the Order stands to the ....Society. I feel more than satisfied since I got in touch with you."

As to whether we are connected with any ....Society, the answer is that we are not. However, we feel we are in spiritual touch with everything in every society that is truly of the Christ and is truly working out what the Wisdom Religion really teaches. Quite naturally, since the Wisdom Religion is not confined to any society, but is broadcasted over the Earth for all who can connect themselves with the higher realms, to receive and give out, there would be a great deal of similarity of philosophy between us and the ....Society.

This Order is not an organization at all: it is simply a Fellowship presenting an exposition of the Wisdom Religion, according to our best interpretation of the

Teachings given us from the Masters or, let us say, the Wisdom Religion as applied to the present-day conditions of the world, not hampered or held back by the interpretations of this same Wisdom Religion which were needed and necessary for an earlier day and a different race. For if it be truly the Wisdom Religion, then, like an overflowing stream of living water, it is forever gushing forth anew so that all peoples, races and minds may drink and be refreshed; that they may absorb this living water according to their mental capacity and get just the help they need. Therefore, let us say, we drink of this living water at its source and we pass it on.

We make no personal claims, but all who find the Water of Life which we are passing on, good and sweet and true and helpful in their lives, are welcome to drink. And in so far as the . . . . Society or any other society draws from the same stream, even tho they express it a little differently, just so far are we united with them and no farther.

> "In our very near surroundings we have seen many examples of people giving nearly all their time to higher studies, but alas! forgetting that they had to fulfill many daily duties. Such neglect of obvious duties may seem to them, at their stage of evolution, to be right, but with it we cannot agree."
>
> July 10, 1923.

We agree with you entirely as to the necessity of performing one's duty in the world and to one's children and family, but we think you have quite misunderstood our pamphlet if you think—as your letter seems to imply—that to study with us would take you away from such duties or require a large part of your time. On the contrary, the short lesson sent out each month takes only a few moments to read, although since it is very meaty as to its contents, its teachings should be thought over and meditated upon as often as possible during the month. This can be done, however, at odd times when your mind and attention is not required for outer things, such times as while walking to and from work, on a street car—instead of reading a newspaper—as a subject for family discussion, etc.

The Teachings therefore require very little time in the sense of study hours definitely set aside for that purpose. The main thing is that the ideas presented should be hovering and digesting in the background of the mind a great part of the time, so that at times of action, expression or emergency they will come into manifestation as the ideals and motives of your thoughts and actions almost before you have time to think.

It is often a great mistake to attempt to devote one's entire attention to the study of metaphysical and occult or spiritual subjects unless one's life-work is that of a teacher of such subjects. That idea is a relic of the medieval days when the highest ideal of leading the spiritual life or seeking spiritual development was to withdraw from the world into monasteries and convents and devote all one's time to "saving one's Soul"—which is immortal and needs no "saving," in the orthodox sense of being damned from birth until "saved."

Quite apart from the spiritual selfishness of such a practice and the spiritual pride thus engendered—"I am holier than thou," etc.—the person so doing had practically to run away from the duties and responsibilities of life in the environment in which he had incarnated, and therefore lost the experiences, great lessons and Soul-unfoldment which he otherwise would have gained.

What is the obvious lesson from these so widely prevailing conditions? We maintain that it is that man is intended to unfold and manifest his spiritual development *right in the environment where the Great Law leads him* in the various epochs of his life. And our whole Teachings are an effort to show man how he can thus unfold his true spiritual nature in the midst of his everyday affairs, and thus help on the evolution of all the world by radiating to everything he contacts, in all worlds, and kingdoms, the degree of spiritual radiation he has been able to manifest.

From the above you will see that you do not have to neglect any duty or give up your work in the world, leave any church or society with which you may be connected, so long as it really helps you, or postpone to some future incarnation studying with us; for our work is a personal one and not that of an organization, hence makes no requirements or demands upon you; you yourself make your own conditions and your own response according to your reaction from within.

We trust that you will not interpret this letter as urging you to study with us, for we want only those who have a strong inner urge to do so, but rather an effort to correct your viewpoint with regard to our work, whether you feel the inner call to join us or not.

> "The strange way I was divinely led to a knowledge of your wonderful Order makes me know better the meaning of the words, "When the pupil is ready, the Teacher appears."

We are indeed glad that you have realized the Divine Truth that "When the pupil is ready the Teacher appears." We have never known this to fail, but there are many people who cannot understand. They think it means that some Teacher in the physical, some Master who will come to them and give them some magical personal power. And it is largely because of this almost universal misinterpretation of this precept that there are so many teachers today who are calling themselves Masters and masquerading as capable of fulfilling this axiom.

In reality, the Teacher who appears is just the thing that can teach us to take the next step. Sometimes it is a friend quite as ordinary as ourselves; another time it is a book, another an incident in our lives. But it is always just that thing which teaches us to take the next step. We are very glad that in your case it was one of our books which brought you into close touch with this Order and the Teacher back of this Order.

> "I am a . . . . and do not know if I am doing right in studying with you."
> Dec. 2, 1922.

We can only say that this Order is not an organization, hence is not something you "join" in the ordinary sense of being bound to it. It is a gathering into an universal fold of all who desire its Teachings and feel they are helped thereby, no matter what their beliefs or other affiliations. It makes no difference as far as we are concerned. We carefully abstain from criticism of any other teachings, religion, sect or movement, and we gladly help all who come to us, no matter what religion, society or organization they may belong to. However, if you find that your . . . . Society is less broad and tolerant and objects to your receiving the Teachings of this Order, then you yourself must choose between the two according to the dictates of your own Inner Guidance. Ask earnestly in prayer for that Guidance and follow it.

"I got to know your books tome time ago. Each came to me at the right time and I must say wonderfully. I had declined to follow the . . . . Society or the . . . . in Europe, though they had helped me on a great deal for some time. It was Jesus and His teachings that I wanted. I wanted to write to you and ask for help but something prevented me. After many struggles I felt now quite suddenly that I might ask now, something pushes me to do so. I hope I am not misguided."

Sept 3, 1922.

Your letter is very convincing, for it shows you are really following the guidance of your own inner Divine Self. That which we call the Great White Lodge of Masters, or the Great Ones, always teach their pupils to follow their own Divine Guidance no matter how difficult the struggle.

Also, the fact of having passed through the . . . . Society and other schools of thought and finding that altho they helped you they still did not satisfy you, is another proof of the same thing. For it is only as we try everything that appeals to us and extract from each that which really feeds us that we make ourselves ready for advanced advice and help. We are all like a little seed planted in the ground which must seek for its food down in the dark earth and learn to find just the necessary nourishment for its growth. And only when it puts up a shoot above ground can the gardener come and train it and help it in its positive growth. This is why you felt suddenly that the time had come to write us. In other words, the little shoot had put up above ground and it was time for the gardener to come and help train it, or help to tie it temporarily to a stake which would make it grow straight and strong and able to resist the storms of life.

All we can say to you in regard to your questioning as to whether you have made a mistake or not is that we will do our best to interpret to you our Teachings. And after you have grown and reached the strength where you no longer need any help, you will know it, even as you knew when to write. But as long as our help, or rather the help sent to you through us, is a real help, hold fast to it. Gather from it every ounce of living force that is in this way transferred to you and be thankful and know well that your heavenly Father knows what is best; knows how to guide you to food suitable for every stage of your growth. Therefore "Take, eat; for verily this is my body," saith the Christ, *i.e.*, every spiritual food that helps you onward and upward is the body of the Christ, to be eaten and digested and lived upon. And when it no longer helps, then something else will be provided.

However, you will find, as do so many, that as your needs grow, so will the Teachings grow, or in other words, that as you are guided to draw closer to this Order and to ask more Soul-searching questions, so will the answers come and so will you receive the divine help that grows with your growth and provides for your ongoing day by day and year by year.

> "As I examined my own inclinations and found them so strongly in favor of your Teachings, it seemed to me that perhaps my wish to believe in the truth of them was rooted in a selfish wish. I do not want to believe in things merely because I personally am inclined to them. I want to know the truth regardless of whether it pleases me or not."

As to your fear lest believing in the truth of your inner conviction might be but a selfish desire to gratify that which would give you happiness, note well that exactly as in everything that grows there is a tiny germ of life which is Divine, which makes even the little seed planted in the dark ground struggle to gather to itself exactly the particles needed for its growth; which makes the seed keep on growing and growing until it is firmly rooted and able to put up its shoots above ground, so in every human heart there is this divine knowledge that the God of Love has impregnated the soil of its life, or let us say, the surrounding circumstances of its life, with exactly the conditions which will make it strong. Then it finds that every struggle helps it to take root more deeply, and finally through this rooting and the discriminating following of the Divine Instinct, at last it will put up a spiritual shoot into the sunshine. Then it will find the corroboration of all its inner convictions. It will find that while underground it may have dreamed that the Sun shone and the rain fell and the wind blew and that flowers did blossom and grow, but now after its long struggle it has at last proved that all this is true.

Therefore, one of the most convincing yet mystical sayings is that the Soul must grow as the flower grows, silently yet surely opening its heart to the Spiritual Sun. But at first the Sun must be but the reflection of the divine immortal Spiritual Light which "lighteth everyone that cometh into the world," which shines deep within its own heart. Only as the Soul thus follows this Light and keeps on struggling will the proof ultimately come to it that indeed it is all true.

The things you are personally inclined to are the things you cannot help believing, but commonsense says that you must put them to the proof. Things in the outer life you are inclined to believe may or may not be true, but the inner mysteries of the Soul to which you feel yourself inclined you may depend upon. For they come from this Inner Light which is given you to lead you into that which is especially needed for your Soul's growth.

> "I am writing because of cheering news of tiny seed sprouts of interest in the Order appearing above the surface. Rev. . . . . ., pastor of . . . ., and Mr. and Mrs. . . . . . find in your books a philosophy of the heart appealing to them and instructive in a profound sense. His class of boys from 17 to 20 in the . . . . Sunday School are deeply interested in *The Voice of Isis*, which he uses in his class. May we have a word from you to our little gathering that the sprouts may produce leaves, blossoms and finally a full harvest of fruit?"
>
> Nov. 3, 1922.

Your letter brings with it a great joy, for it shows that this work we are putting forth is spreading in unexpected places. And since receiving your letter there have been several of a similar nature, showing that there are many little classes which are finding great interest in our Teachings and are studying and spreading them. Some of these classes are in churches and one is in the Salvation Army. You are sure to find that your mental house begins to put itself in order and that the door stands wide open, not only for you to give out the Teachings understandingly, but also for the great spiritual power of the Divine to flow in the instant you take up any work to help others in the loving way you have done.

As you go on with this work you will find greater power to see the hidden forces and to bring them to the surface. Religion has all in it that is needed for the helpfulness of humanity, but humanity is so lacking in understanding, and also many of the teachings have been given out in such a way that they seem to perpetuate misunderstanding instead of helping on the development of a true spiritual understanding of the matter. Indeed we have reached the point where religion must be analyzed. Man will no longer take guess work and fairy tales for true Science, nor will he much longer try to satisfy his spiritual hunger in the same way, for he has reached his mental majority. We must emphasize more and more strongly the necessity of asking that the vital touch with the Divine shall become a personal experience, a living reality within us; that our mental powers shall be turned toward it and understand it and take fearlessly all that it brings us. Then we will have no fear of any misunderstanding or any lack of work.

> "I am proud to know that I have been enrolled as a student and am at last affiliated with a circle through which I can give my best expression for Good. For I can give my best only through that organization which embodies that all important spirit of loving kindness. In so many others we find the key-note of love and sympathy giving way to cold intellectuality. Will I digress by continuing my daily study of Madam Blavatsky's *Secret Doctrine*?"
>
> Dec 7, 1922.

We are very glad of your appreciation of the Order and we are sure that it indicates that you have touched the heart of things and know what to look for. It is not that we feel we are superior to all others, for we know there are many avenues of Truth each fitted to those who are its followers, but nevertheless it gives us great joy to find a student here and there who really touches the heart of this Order and finds that which the heart of the Order feels is the most necessary of all things to give out.

Not only do you not digress or diminish your efficiency by studying *The Secret Doctrine*, but it is a very great help in your studies, as we quote from it extensively.

> "I haven't my feet on the Path yet but I hope by diligent study now to be able to start on it early in life in my next incarnation."
>
> July 28, 1922.

Dear student, you are on the Path the very instant you make up your mind to take the first step. There are many steps on the Path and we are on it just as soon as we determinedly step out and decide to go on by the strength and power of the Christ.

> "I have been a student of occultism for a number of years, having been connected with the Center for four years. I spent a year at . . . . and left there a physical wreck. From all the organizations and isms I have learned some invaluable lessons, but there still seems to be a lack, a great need which I seem unable to supply alone."
>
> Dec. 14, 1922.

We think that the thing of which you feel such a great need and which you cannot find in any of the various "isms" you have been looking into, is really the touch of Divine Love and understanding. And this we as an Order have tried to make our leading characteristic. We want you to understand fully, however, that it is not in any way dependent on the personality of the Founders, but is a real positive ray of force sent into this Order, as it is into the heart of each one open to it, from the Great Ones who are the forerunners of the coming Great Teacher. Their work is especially to gather in those Souls who have studied and sought, yet have not found the direct heart-touch from this coming One which can make them ready to devote their lives, not merely to the study of the philosophy, altho this is very necessary, but to the study of real co-operation and devotion.

Therefore in this Order we put love, devotion, co-operation and true facing of one's self as the first requisites to real inner affiliation. We have tried to provide every opportunity for our students to find out just how to face themselves and how to find out just what it is that is holding them back. And this takes a truly earnest and determined student to face and apply.

So we give you this little warning and invite you to enter into our ranks, because there is such a great need of persons who are willing to face their hidden faults; to be true to themselves and to co-operate with those who are seeking to reincarnate on this Earth the early fundamental religious truths which have deteriorated and been, as it were, snowed under by manmade forms and creeds. But they must be revived and must find a certain number, be it few or many, who can once more radiate the true ideals of religion and thus form a nucleus which can welcome with sincere heart and worship Him who is to come.

> "Let us form a Universal Federation or League of . . . . *and kindred societies* with its international Bureau, its international Bulletin and its regularly recurring World Congress. Great would be our mutual gain and the gain of the world; . . . . not that the different Societies would abandon their own special lines of work. They would continue as heretofore, ever deepening their inner studies, ever broadening and enriching their outer realizations. But they would no more look askance at each other; they would know and feel their innate brotherhood."
>
> July 11, 1921.

The subject of your letter is one that has been dear to our hearts ever since the beginning of our work, and we have taken every opportunity to promote it. In 1913 a correspondence was started by Mr. . . . . . of the . . . . looking toward a similar federation and we gave it our hearty endorsement and promised our full co-operation when needed, but we have heard nothing further from it. Another Mr. . . . . . has also made some tentative remarks toward a similar end. More recently another . . . . attempt was made by another . . . . Society, but as they planned not to invite any of the. . . . . Societies to participate we refused to co-operate on such a narrow basis, although urgently solicited.

The question of co-operation among spiritual teachers is truly a fundamental one, for since no one presentation of Truth can satisfy all types of mind, all the Societies that are true to spiritual principles are needed. And in these days of DEMONSTRATION, and not mere theory, it is the only thing that will impress the public. If the leaders of societies which teach Brotherhood and Co-operation for the good of all mankind cannot DEMONSTRATE their teachings by manifesting brotherhood and co-operating with others in the same field, they cannot hope to be taken seriously or even be considered sincere outside their own ranks by the great mass of those who are dissatisfied with former teachings and who are hungrily examining every morsel of spiritual food offered and who are eagerly seeking some avenue big enough and broad enough and which can *demonstrate* its ideals in a practical way, which will satisfy their inner heart hunger for real spiritual food presented in an impersonal way.

The . . . . followers, who are considered by many as babes in spiritual and occult philosophy, have already shown us the way with their International Alliance, in which they have managed to federate on a practical working basis the most heterogeneous and diverse elements of mental science. And if they can accomplish this—not without modification, change and growth it is true—why should not those more advanced movements, whose leaders are blessed with a close touch with and direct inspiration from the great Masters of Wisdom, do at least as well?

If it is in order, please present to the Convention the fraternal greetings of *The Order of Christian Mystics*, together with our best wishes for a most fruitful session. May it take the first step toward an International Fellowship of Spiritual Truth Societies which shall accomplish a great work for the demonstration of their principles and the enlightenment of humanity. We, of the O. C. M., not only endorse, but assure you of our hearty support and co-operation in any such movement.[1]

> "I am hoping that I may have the pleasure of forming a little class for reading the Teachings of the Order. I always put in a word of teaching when the opportunity offers, but people are so very conservative here that anything unorthodox is so unwelcome that I hesitate to ask anyone to study with me."
>
> Aug. 17, 1922.

As to getting others to study with you, why not set aside an evening and sit down for an hour and read by yourself? Also repeat the prayers of the Order and after saying them add a personal prayer in which you ask that if there is anyone in your vicinity who can be helped by reading with you, or who can help you, that such a one be sent to you. We have known this to work out in many cases in a wonderful way and therefore recommend it. But you must also hold the thought that if no one comes it is because there is no one who can conveniently be sent to you. However, make this evening a sacred

---

[1] No answer was received to this letter.

one for reading and study even if you are all alone, and always send out that little prayer or, let us say, the invitation for anyone who can be sent.

> "Do you think we are wise in our study class to study the books of others on the same line? Some of the members think it causes confusion and that we should stick to your Teachings, since the class was formed for that purpose."

In any teaching, for instance, were you taking up the study of music, of mathematics or any science, you would choose your Teacher and would stick to that system of teaching until you were thoroughly familiar with it. Then afterward you could judge fairly any other teaching because you had mastered the fundamental principles. It is the same with spiritual teachings. So we say it is wise to choose your avenue and stick to it until you have become familiar with all the fundamentals of its teachings.

If our students would grasp this idea they would save themselves a great deal of wasted mental effort in trying to correlate different teachings. And they would surely save the Founders of this Order much unnecessary work in trying to explain things which would be very simple if the students had applied the same law to the study of occult matters that they would to the study of any other science. Always try to remember the words of Jesus: "By their works ye shall know them." All are good for some, but each one must decide which is best for him, as he would when choosing a wife, for just as each has his Soul-mate, also each has his avenue of truth or Soul-home through which he can best find help, comfort and enlightenment.

Concerning the O. C. M.

> "We have started a small study class, taking up the study of your books and lessons. Do you believe this to be wise or permissible, or shall we wait until we are further advanced?"
> June 3, 1922.

If you make a true center of force, even if it be but two or three who are gathered together in the name of the Living Christ, and if you are truly trying to radiate His great Light, then the forces of the Order will fill you and flow out from you to all around and will make of your little center a radiant Light which shall lighten all who come into its aura. Do not wait until you have gained great wisdom or occult knowledge. The quickest way to gain it is to begin at once and do the best you can.

> "I am puzzled to know why your teachings on the sex of a person differ somewhat from that given out by the . . . . Society, especially as both seem to largely emanate from the same source."
> July 13, 1922.

We can only repeat what we have maintained for so long, *i.e.*, that we are responsible only for our own Teachings, not for those of any other. We feel very sure that we are in touch with the Higher Teachers and if we did not believe, or rather *know* that our Teachings are correct we would not give them out. We are, however, perfectly willing that every one else shall have the privilege of interpreting the Teachings according to his best understanding. All we ask of our pupils is to exercise their own intuition and judge which interpretation seems the most reasonable, then to follow that one.

We know only too well that that which is often called inspiration is the broadcasting from the Great White Lodge of a stream of knowledge or wisdom. Each person capable of reaching up to that point contacts this stream of wisdom, but each must use his own individual brain consciousness to interpret it to the best of his ability. We call the *Bible* an inspired book and we know that many teachers are trying to make it the basis of their teaching, yet because their minds differ there are many differences in the way of interpretation, and each Soul must accept only that with which his own inner Divine Self correlates and declares to be good. We can never say to any one that only that which we give out is true and that which another gives out is false. All we can say to any of our pupils is, "You have within you the power of the Christ to unfold your natural wisdom and can interpret all things in His name."

> "Should one curb the intense desire to tell of wonderful truths revealed through the Order, and offer them only where they are likely to be appreciated, or should one spread them regardless?"
>
> May 2, 1922.

We should use very great discretion, for there are some things which, if told to outsiders, do more harm than good. They either bring forth ridicule and a consequent degradation of our truths, or they bring to the person who is not ready to accept these truths such a great test that he would reject them entirely and by thus rejecting them would bring upon himself karmic retribution in which we would take part, because by giving them to him we were partly responsible.

Every truth revealed to us is a sacred gift and we are held strictly responsible for it. By the word revealed we mean that our mind must conceive of such a truth and must understand it; it must mean something in our lives and not be merely an intellectual conception. If we cast our pearls before swine they will surely trample them in the mire and turn and rend us. This rending is not a bodily one, but is of the inner spiritual understanding of truth, and we are responsible for every pearl of wisdom we have thus cast before those capable of trampling it in the mire.

> "Wish to thank you most sincerely—and to express my appreciation of the most extraordinary grasp you display of this vast subject: occult wisdom. You have met my inquiry as to your attainments with a most generous attitude of freedom and I am still rubbing my eyes in amazement at the disclosures you are making of such transcendent import. It certainly evidences more than human wisdom.
>
> "Am I correct in assuming that esoteric teaching was first introduced into the country in 1876 through H. P. B. and Mrs. . . . . and that from these have sprung the various other interpretations?"
>
> May 29, 1922.

You are right when you see in the reply to your letter, wisdom more than mortal and a grasp of the great subject which is quite different from that of most so called teachers who depend entirely upon their own wisdom and who are trammeled by the limitation of world thought. As to the leaders of this movement, they have been chosen by the great Lodge of Masters, not because of any super-human power but simply because through long training they have been perfected in the power to transmit truly, and with humility and a willing obedience to obliterate the personality and thus to give out only that which comes through from the Great White Lodge.

As to your query regarding esoteric teachings having been introduced into this country through H. P. B. and Mrs. . . . . , both H. P. B. and in a lesser way

Mrs. . . . . were just what the transmitters of the messages of this Order are today, transmitters of the truths which are being poured out for humanity. These truths are forever being poured out by the Great Ones, but the transmitters are responsible for the clarity and purity of the avenues through which they are given to the world. There is always a personal quality which cannot help entering in, for inspiration is not as so many think, a literal dictation, word for word, from some Teacher on the higher plane, but a broadcasting of Divine Wisdom which is received and interpreted according to the development and ability of those who can receive it.

> "Will you kindly give me some idea as to in what way your Teachings surpass those of the . . . ., and why there should be different expressions of one Divine Teaching?"
> Sept. 3, 1922.

We note that you have passed through various schools of instruction and we know this is as it should be, for all avenues of spiritual help are put forth to feed and help certain types of mentality and only when we find the one that really helps us are we sure we have found the truth for ourselves. Therefore those who find in *The Order of Christian Mystics* the help they are seeking will also find that it makes no claims of being the only avenue of truth; but that it does claim to be one avenue of giving forth the great messages of life from the great Lodge of Masters in the language and manner which to them, the Christian Mystics, seem the most helpful. We know full well that there are many people who require a different way of receiving truth, but to those who are ready for our Teachings this is the best way. Those who accept our Teachings with joy and satisfaction seem to seek no farther, because they have found their spiritual home.

> "I thank you ever so much for the loving letter I received. I know not how I can express the gratitude I feel toward the Order and its leaders, for what it has done for me in this one short year in which I have had the privilege of belonging to it. One question: As to tobacco, I realize that it will have to go, but am at a loss which is the best way to get rid of it."
>
> April 4, 1922.

As to smoking in moderation, it is occultly not objectionable in itself, but anything at all which becomes a habit is bad. Tobacco has a disinfecting force and in many respects is not objectionable if used absolutely under the control of your own will and only at times when it is really needed. But it must not become a habit. It is just as bad to form a habit of overeating as of smoking. And the moment anything becomes a habit it is time to stop it. The continued and persistent use of tobacco is deleterious to the nervous system and the only time it is permissible is when under great nervous strain, especially with supersensitive persons who need a little extra stimulus to carry them over periods of such strain.

As to tobacco cures, we cannot say that we have any confidence in them. Often the cures are worse than the disease, although there may, of course, be exceptions to this rule. As to suggestions before going to sleep, yes, this would be helpful if they are given in the name of the living Christ and if you call upon all those helpers on the higher planes who can and do work with the Christ and whose desire is to help and assist you in breaking the habit. In fact, the instant you get to the point where you realize your own Selfhood and your supreme control over all your faculties and ideals; the instant you realize that nobody and no thing can affect you unless you permit it in your aura, then you can cure yourself of all habits.

> "Such a magnificent man as Mr. . . . . . expressed regret that since your writings seem to be based entirely on . . . ., why should such teachings emanate from any other source than the original centers? Why so many different sources of teaching the same truths?"
>
> July 24, 1922.

We are glad you have found in us and in the Teachings of this Order a deep understanding and broad tolerance for the teachings of others. We hope this understanding will never be lessened, but that time will bring you into a greater realization that these are the underlying principles upon which we are striving to build up this work.

We know there are men of many minds and each must be touched in his own way, yet we are quite ready to leave all that to the wisdom of the Divine Leader and Guide of this mighty work. All who are familiar with the inner mysteries should be joined heart and hand and Soul to bring these truths before the world in every reasonable way which will really help. Each mind must have them presented in its own way, just as each person must have the kind of food his own taste demands. We cannot all eat the same things or receive the same nourishment or satisfaction from them. Even if we could, some like theirs prepared and served in one way and some in another.

Why such a "magnificent man," as you call Mr. . . . ., should regret that since our writings are based upon the . . . .sources, we do not work within their ranks, this is easily seen, because of the following our Teachings have attained. You must remember that the sources of the . . . .are, as they purport to be, the essence of Divine Wisdom, that

Divine Wisdom which has no limit. It is like a mighty radiophone broadcasted through the world and all who have the receiving apparatus can and should receive it and express it to the best of their ability. The very fact, therefore, that these sources can be traced in more than one expression of Truth simply proves that they are true, that they have been broadcasted and received by all who can "tune in."

There is no limit to Divine Wisdom. Inspiration is simply the result of the flowing outward of a mighty spiritual radiant force which every one who has sufficiently perfected his own mind and has prepared himself to receive, can receive; but each must express it according to his own ability. Every mind and every force which is expressed in the lesser universe of man is provided for. The instant any of us become fixed or grooved or begin to say "We are the only ones who can receive this radiographic inspiration," at once we disconnect our antenna and find that little that is new can reach us. The more, however, we recognize the universality of this force, the more the antennae spread and widen, that much more truth can be received through them.

As to restraining yourself and sticking fast to but one interpretation at a time, this is indeed a very important thing to do, but before you do this you should have tried all that attracts you. As St Paul says, "Prove all things and hold fast that which is good." In other words, we are not like wandering atoms in space with no guidance, no power of grasping and understanding Truth, but we have been put here with all the powers of the universe touching us and manifesting through us. We have been created with a perfect receiving apparatus by which we can not only receive the great radio-dispensing of Divine Wisdom and Truth, but can separate it and judge it. For we have had written for us in an unmistakable way the great Book of Nature. We are told from the beginning that only those things we see worked out in Nature are and can be truths, and that man is the microcosm of the macrocosm and hence must follow the same laws. And if he does he will find the same satisfactory results. Therefore, we can only say to you that nothing is true to you, be it ever so true to others, unless you can prove it for yourself; unless you can see its corresponding accomplishment worked out for you in the Cosmos and can prove it from the laws of Nature or your own experience.

As to finding dissimilarity in the various teachings, if you look at Nature you will find wonderful dissimilarity in the flora and fauna of the various countries and localities. Even in one single locality how many various kinds of things must grow in the same environment, yet how the forces that are needed to support life in these various things are fitted for them! There is no such thing as exact identity or monotony in the whole world. That which we call Ancient Wisdom could be better expressed as Everlasting Truth, and no truth that becomes ancient can be helpful to the generation that is newly born or just coming into its day of manifestation until it is reinterpreted in terms which that nation can comprehend. Yet the ancient truths contain Divine Principles upon which can be built up that which is helpful to each New Day.

The trouble with you, dear student, is that you are looking constantly and continually for Teachers outside of yourself; for those who claim to know more; for those whom you consider more fitted than you to grasp Truth. Yet the truth of it is that although there are many who have studied and have grasped perhaps more of the truth than you have or who have meditated and assimilated more, nevertheless each Soul has within it the great receiving station for this Divine Wisdom. And while we must study, yet we must always refer all to our inner Divine Self and accept only that which rings true to us. If you are constantly looking outside of yourself no wonder you are lost in the maze of differences and claims. But if you are looking within you will find that all these differences are summed up and interpreted in the mystic music of the spheres and are given out to you in a simple way, the way that you can best grasp and understand.

There are certain laws by which we know that Nature in all its mystic and marvelous diversity can be harmonized basically. It is just so with man. First, the thing we are striving to study must show itself to be helpful. It must manifest in our character and above all things, in tolerance, broadness, gentleness and love. If it does not, then, although we know there may be and must be *some* truth at the bottom of the well, yet why bother to clean out the well when we have so much that is beautiful and helpful outside of it? And we know that in due time all will be made clean if the pure stream of living water is bubbling up in the well. All that we need for our ongoing and help will be brought to us and we shall be able to grasp and understand it.

> "Please give me your opinion of the value of Eastern Teachings as compared with Western Occultism for Americans."
>
> May 12, 1922.

Replying to your question as to the essential differences between Christian Mysticism or the spiritual philosophy of the West and that of the East, we would say that die differences spring largely from the point of view, which in turn is influenced by the characteristics of their respective Race-thought.

The objects of both schools are the same, namely, the realization, unfoldment and manifestation of the Divine Indweller in man while he is still living here on earth, but the methods of this attainment are quite opposite. The Eastern schools seek this end through withdrawal from the world and all its activities, the killing out or devitalizing of the personality—often to the extremes of starvation and mutilation—and concentration on the perfection of the self. Christian Mysticism, on the other hand, seeks to manifest its ideals through being in the world although not ruled by it, and concentrating on the perfect meeting of its conditions through reliance upon the guidance of the indwelling Higher Self.

The ideal of the Eastern schools seems to be that the object of all our devotions, strivings and aspirations should be to seek "liberation" from the responsibilities of life in the world, from the desires of the flesh and from the Wheel of Karma. The viewpoint of Christian Mysticism is that however desirable such ideals may seem to the individual they are separative instead of unitive and therefore seem to us but an exalted form of selfishness.

Instead of concentrating all our efforts upon withdrawing and leaving the world behind and seeking our own perfection and salvation, without regard to how the rest of the world is getting along or what hardships our withdrawal might impose upon others, Christian Mysticism teaches us to seek union with and the conscious guidance of the Higher Self (Atman), not that we may get away from the world, but to perfect ourselves in every way—body, mind and Spirit—for service in and to the world. In other words, instead of despising the body and seeking to kill out the personality, we seek to perfect it in every way that it may be a more perfect instrument through which the Divine in us (the Higher Self or Soul) can express itself more fully and helpfully, not for our own satisfaction and happiness alone, but that through the more perfect expression and radiation of its Divine Consciousness, Divine Life-force and Divine Powers it may teach, both by precept and example, the less-evolved ones who suffer so pitifully through their ignorance, how to meet the trials, tests and conditions of every-day life in the world with the proper attitude of mind and with the right understanding of them, so as to learn the lessons from every experience and turn all "to the glory of God" or to the greater manifestation of the Divine in us and the world as a whole.

Instead of despising the body and seeking to kill out its functions and desires we seek their perfect control, not through devitalizing them by fasting, etc., but through mastery of them under the guidance of the Higher Self, so that each and all can be used for their highest ends. We regard the perfection of the body and the cultivation of the personality as an important part of the Soul's mission on earth, for without it the Soul could not find expression or accomplish its mission in matter. Therefore we hold that there is no attribute, function, organ or part of body or mind that is not needed for the Soul's perfect expression on earth; for since they were all given us by our Creator, they must be necessary to the purpose for which we were manifested on earth. But instead of seeking for their development as an end—as the physical culturists the body and the mental scientists the mind—we seek their perfection merely as a means to the end, namely, that we may have a more perfect instrument. Hence we seek their perfect control or mastery, so that they shall not be used for self-indulgence, but for their normal and highest ideal ends, to the glory of God.

We hold that if the object of all attainment were to get away from the world we would far better not have incarnated in it at all! For then we would not have to take the trouble to get away from the very place where the Great Law has placed us! But since the Law of Divine Manifestation requires us to incarnate, there must be some great end to be attained thereby. What is the object of our incarnation? To get away from it as soon as possible? Obviously not. No, the object of incarnation is to build up and perfect an organism and a personality which shall be in very truth "a Temple of the living God," as the *Bible* tells us it should be. In other words, to make a perfect, strong, responsive and obedient servant which the Higher Self can the better work through to accomplish its mission in this world of form and matter. For we hold that the Earth was created as a theatre upon whose stage is to be worked out an advanced step in the unfoldment of humanity without whose advance the globe itself can never reach its perfection.

While we do recognize that when certain higher faculties and functions reach a particular stage of development it is advisable for the candidate to withdraw from the excitement and distractions of the world to some place of peace and quiet for a time, nevertheless this applies only to very advanced disciples who necessarily are few in number and whose necessary conditions constitute the exception and not the rule for humanity in general. But even in those cases the retirement lasts only until certain faculties and powers have been developed and control of them gained, which faculties and powers will enable them to be still more helpful to their fellowmen. Whereupon it is their duty to return to the world and teach.

This being the Law of Life, if such advanced disciples refuse to help the less evolved, in their next life they must inevitably reincarnate in the midst of the classes and conditions which they refused to help and thus find themselves with all their higher ideals, powers and sensitized bodies held in the vortex of the world's most hampering conditions until they are forced to take up the task they refused to accept lest they impede their own development. Examples of yogis and devotees of various kinds incarnated under such conditions can easily be pointed out, and their lot is surely not an enviable one.

To sum up, in our school of Western Mysticism we follow, not the Path of Renunciation of the world so universally followed in the East, but the Path of Service in and to the world; the Path of Recognition and Tolerance.

Chapter VI

AFTER DEATH CONDITIONS

"Do you favor cremation? How many days should elapse after death before a person is buried or cremated?"

May 23, 1922.

After the life has apparently left the body it should be carefully preserved a day or two until some sign of decay is seen. The time varies much according to the age of the person and also the disease which has taken him off. However, you can generally tell when the time for cremation has arrived by the discolorations under the finger nails or in any part of the body, also by the odor.

We certainly do believe in cremation, as it breaks the link between the corpse and the astral body and permits the astral body to join the Higher Self rather than to cling to the old corpse. However, when a person is old he or she is generally tired of life and does not desire to linger, so that unless he is very much attached to physical life and very strong willed, an elderly person will generally drop to sleep after passing out. While this sleep endures, if someone who understands calls for those helpers on the other side who understand such conditions and who in response to such calls take the astral body to a place where the person can sleep without interruption and can be watched over, the person will have dreams which are like experiences and which teach him many things almost as completely as tho he were living through them. And when such a person wakes up he is often quite advanced. But this would not be simply because of the passing from the physical into the astral. It is also sometimes possible for persons in this dream state apparently to appear to those they have left behind, but if we know how to distinguish we will know it is but a dream consciousness and not the persons themselves.

Do not use any ice until you are sure that the Spirit has really left the body. It is seldom necessary to have the body embalmed if cremation is to take place.

When one like your mother who is quite old begins to fail in health and in mind it is generally because the Soul is beginning to separate from the body. In such cases there is seldom much of the Soul left to depart at death, as most of the higher consciousness has joined itself to the Real Self before the end really came. This is not a thing to grieve you, for if you understand that her mental lapses are simply because her mind has been called up into the higher planes, you should rejoice rather than otherwise. It should also give you great patience, knowing that little is left except what we call the animal consciousness or the mentality of the physical body, or "second childhood."

Truly the modern funeral, concentrating on sorrow, loss and death, is an ordeal and is one of the ordeals we hope will ultimately be done away with. For when we believe there is really no death, but that life is continuous, there will be a rejoicing over the release from suffering of any Soul who passes on. In fact these funerals are links which bind the Soul to Earth, for few can resist the tremendous pulling force such a funeral has over them. And they partake of all the unhappiness of those left behind and of all the thoughts sent out of the awfulness of it; whereas if left alone they would look upon it as a happy release.

"Do deceased persons suffer when an autopsy is performed soon after death?"
Oct 10, 1923.

At least three days should elapse between the death and the autopsy. If the autopsy is performed too soon the deceased does suffer, for it should not be performed until the Soul has completely withdrawn from the body. However, those who know and are striving to live close to the divine loving Godhead can ask their loving Father before passing out that they shall be taken immediately away from the body, for they should be perfectly willing to leave the body and all earthly ties and go direct to Him. They must make up their minds in a determined way that they have said goodbye to all that is earthly and not permit anything to hold them to their bodies. Then they will pass away immediately when the last breath is drawn. But if they cling to earthly desires or even stand close to their bodies because they think they cannot leave the body; or if they are trying to comfort the sorrow of someone left behind, then when the autopsy takes place they may feel the astral effect of it, and that is far more severe than the physical one.

Therefore when you are talking to people regarding transition tell them of the great joy of waking up in their Father's presence and of saying good-bye to their bodies and to the Earth just as quickly as possible, not permitting any ties to hold them to it. Then there need be no fear of pain. Even those who have already passed out, if they permit themselves to hang on to earth conditions because they feel sympathy and sorrow for their loved ones left behind, will suffer with those left behind.

The one thing we should like to teach the whole world is that once you have drawn your last breath on Earth you should be done with Earth; that the door is open to a higher realm and that the loving Father Mother is waiting to welcome you into this higher realm and bring you its great joys. The duties that await you are not duties connected with Earth at all; those are able to wait until your next incarnation when you will take them up once more and bear the Karma of them, having mentally learned what they really are and what the Karma is; consequently not permitting it to cause as much suffering as it would through ignorance. This is the great lesson we ask you to help us teach.

Remember Earth is one sphere and heaven another. It matters not whether you have always obeyed Divine Law or have made many mistakes; nevertheless having drawn your last breath, for a time at least you are done with Earth. Get away from it and depend on your Divine Father-Mother to give you the new lessons needed. If you have been wicked, as the world calls it, these new lessons will not be of suffering, but will teach you why you have failed and how to overcome it in the next life. And when you take up earth-life once more the opportunity will be given you to make it right, and in the times of temptation and sorrow and trial there will come over you a memory of the lesson learned and the great love that is with you and you can rest in its fullness and its ability to pull you through.

> "I have been recently requested by three Souls from the other side, my wife, my son and my brother, who advised me to join your Order as its teachings would greatly help me to unfold, so that I would be enabled to help humanity in the trials which are foretold as coming."
>
> Nov. 21, 1922.

We are glad to comply with the request which has

been given you by Souls from the other side. This advice is not surprising, for there are many Souls on the other side who recognize and understand the vital work being done by this Order. The whole world is facing grave conditions, and the great work which has been given into the hands of this Order at the present time is to gather together out of all lands and all peoples those who can understand and grasp the vital necessity of changing the world thought from vindictiveness, hatred and unbrotherliness into a vital realization of the necessity of spreading Truth, or as we say in our *Prayer for World Harmony*, "Only as we see ourselves as parts of the one great body of humanity, can peace, harmony, success and plenty descend upon us."

Therefore, we are not trying to develop psychic powers in our pupils at this particular period. We feel that the powers to be developed are the powers of understanding the great necessity of brotherliness or, in other words, the mystic and magical powers of the Christ manifesting in us, which alone can save the whole world from dire catastrophes, wars and horrors unspeakable. Although as a general thing these powers are not classed as mental and psychic powers, nevertheless they are the very acme of such powers. For we can only accomplish such a great task when we touch in consciousness the higher mystic center of God-consciousness which knows all things and recognizes all the peoples of the Earth as one great body of brothers and sisters. For this reason we send out our lessons touching on all kinds of necessary knowledge. But we do not follow the usual so-called psychic development methods. We seek first the kingdom of God and His righteousness, knowing that to touch this Divine Realm the Soul must ascend through all the lower realms, which include every kind of psychic development. But because it is seeking for God-consciousness, the everlasting arms will be around the aspirant; and the hand of the living God will be grasping the hand of the pupil and leading him onward. Therefore it is the Heart Doctrine and devotional method which we advocate as most advantageous.

> "Will you tell me what to do with the belongings of my dear daughter who, as you know, has passed away. She had built up a childish selfishness concerning her belongings and I seem to feel every time I try to use even her wrist watch, etc., that she does not like it. So I have arranged all her things in her room just as she liked them. Is this the best thing to do?"
>
> Sept 13, 1922.

If your daughter had built up a childish selfishness concerning her things, you are certainly fostering it by arranging her room just as she would like it. Try to realize that now that she has passed away from these physical surroundings and is under the guidance and love of the great Teachers, there are greater things for her to learn, and that her happiness will consist in dropping all fondness or longings for earthly conditions. If you arrange the room as you suggest you are making a great magnet which will hold her back, and in all probability she will find it quite impossible to leave that room for some time and will be there constantly trying to enjoy her earthly belongings and being held by them.

This is the usual condition. Many persons are held back for ages just because the things they loved on Earth are carefully preserved. We ourselves know of one case especially—that of an old man who had been on the other side of life for at least two hundred years and yet spent his entire time in arranging his library, which had been preserved, and in handling his old books. This becomes a bitter trial to the one thus held back, for he always feels and knows he should go on.

And the great loving Souls who desire to help them are always seeking to draw such persons up into the higher conditions, yet these earthly belongings make a link which they find it very difficult to break.

We tell you all this because we know that if you once understand the real harm you are doing your daughter by thus holding her back you will not want to do it. It is not the same as being held by a bond of love to you, for this is not to be condemned. One who has passed over will linger beside one he has deeply loved and will find great comfort, and at the same time will be able to make himself at home in the higher realms and to learn the necessary lessons. Such a one can also bring these lessons to the one left behind on Earth. But this is entirely different from the love of *things*, for such a love is selfishness.

Therefore our advice to you is to take her things and make some good use of them. For instance, give any clothes to some one who needs them. Do good with all she has left and as you thus dispose of them offer up a little prayer that the God of Love shall bless both the gift and the giver. Speak to your daughter, knowing she is near and can hear you; tell her you are trying to fulfill the law of love and that you want her to leave behind her not a room full of things, but a blessing; that the things she had cherished in life will bring joy and helpfulness to some one else. And although just at first she may not appreciate it, we are quite sure that in a very short time she will bless you, for all the blessings springing out of the gifts you thus make to others will make a radiant pathway of light for her Soul. It will lead her upward and will give her the great spiritual joy and understanding she so much needs.

> "I have had a regular Job experience, one thing after another in the form of illness. Am wondering if there is a psychic cause. A sister who had been bed-ridden for seven years passed on. She was determined not to die and fought bitterly against death. A psychic friend saw her standing near me. My brother, who passed on a little later, suffered dreadfully with headaches just like those I have."
> Oct. 9, 1922.

It is a terrible thing to fight with death, because it helps death to become a reality. Yet, as you know, there is no death: only a change from a partial life on Earth, where we cannot fully express all that is in us as we would like, to a free and beautiful life where we will find ourselves living in the very essence of harmony and beauty.

If, however, there is any danger of your sister standing near you and throwing her forces over you, all you have to do is to use the challenge. Tell her "in the name of the living Christ," kindly and sweetly, that she *must* stand outside your aura far enough not to throw her influence over you. Also put the *Ring of Protection*[1] around yourself and it will protect you from all harm. However, do not accept the thought that your headaches are of a psychic nature until you have eliminated every possible focus of physical infection which may be lurking in your body. If they are psychic they are easily overcome by challenging.

Remember that this challenge does not necessarily mean a cruel or harsh driving away from us of those we love. It can be given in a loving way, altho it must be positive. Say, "I recognize your presence. I can hear every word you say quite as well outside my aura as in it. I know your love and desire to help me, but you must stand outside my aura, because your pres-

---

[1] See Appendix for the *Prayer of Protection*.

ence within it throws over me those troubles with which you passed over." Then every night and morning and several times a day put the *Ring of Protection* around you, and repeat the little *Prayer of Protection*, and call upon the Christ to fill your whole aura with His Light, your heart with His Truth, and your life with His beauty and radiance.

> "Should we not be ready to make any effort to prevent one from taking his own life? Is not this the unpardonable sin? If the one has lost his mental poise and commits suicide is he equally guilty?"
>
> Aug. 9, 1923.

We know there are teachings regarding suicide which make it seem almost the unpardonable sin; in truth it is descending into the depths where nothing but the cry of the Soul for Light can help. Sometimes this seems to come, as in cases in which persons have lost their mentality through the terrible experiences of war, etc., when it would seem that they are quite innocent. Yet this is never so. Nothing ever comes to us except that which we ourselves have created or correlated with. And in cases where the mentality fails to grasp and understand the higher truths the persons have simply let go at some time in their lives and have let the waves of sorrow and affliction sweep over them. Then the belief in the supremacy of evil and the impotency of good (God) completely fills their hearts and minds.

To prove that it was not the war alone that caused the collapse, we have only to look at the many who passed through the terrible ordeal of war and yet came out better and with a higher understanding of the greatness of the power that sustained them. Whereas those whom we might justly call the weaklings (not weaklings in physical bodies, but in the understanding of Truth) find that all the sophistries built up from the teachings of the church or from their philosophy or their own carelessness and failure to study life's problems, utterly fail, and there is nothing for them to fall back on, therefore the total collapse of mind.

Without special training it is unwise to try to enter into the conditions of such persons. For a suicide and also one who has lost his mentality, or who has lost his responsibility, is in absolute loneliness and darkness. If the untrained try to enter this condition they are apt to become affiliated and overcome by its awfulness and lose their own power to help. But we can cry out in our heart of hearts and also with our lips to our Christ and ask that He shall send to such people the desire for the Light as quickly as possible (it will come ultimately, but we want it to come as quickly as possible). And the instant their Souls cry for Light the Light will be sent to them and the angelic helpers specially trained for such work will minister to them.

> "I lost my poor wife. She did not die a natural death, but in a fit of deep depression, took an overdose of veronal. Can you help me to get her out of the darkness, which is the fate of suicides?"
> Sept 3, 1922.

As to the sad condition in which your wife passed away we would say to you that to concentrate constantly upon her and to let your mind be filled with the awful conditions through which suicides are compelled to pass, is but to emphasize her own conscious realization of the horror of it all. This is because those who pass from physical life through suicide are not far away from the physical plane, for as we have said in our *Realms of the Living Dead* they are shut out of a certain part of the astral world where they would otherwise go through the development necessary for their ongoing, and they are also shut out from their Earth life. They are in a sort of vestibule between the two lives. Therefore, if you concentrate upon it or even pray and hold her constantly in mind, you are drawing her to you and making her longing for Earth life more intense, and the horror of her position more real.

However, in the great scheme of Divine Love which embraces all portions of humanity, those poor creatures who have mistakenly tried to shorten their physical existence are not forgotten. Special arrangements are made for them and there are certain advanced Souls on the higher planes who are specially trained to help them; who go to their assistance and teach them how to progress.

When we desire to help such persons, instead of trying it ourselves or holding them continually in thought, we should simply ask the loving Christ to send them the proper helpers. We have done so in the case of your wife; we have asked that these loving helpers shall seek her out and teach her and lead her into the light. It will also help her if you will say to her in a positive way that the instant she cries for the Light and asks that some one be sent to her, the Light will instantly appear. This is absolutely true, for we have known it to be proved again and again.

So try and put out of your mind the intense sorrow and trouble that is making you practically live in the same atmosphere, even in a darker one than she is enduring. You may depend upon it that help will be sent to her and that she will be taught and her darkness will be lightened and the necessary instruction given to her to bring her into a better understanding of her condition and how to remedy it.

> "Is it possible to meet after death one whom you have wronged and yet whom you dearly love, and is it possible to ask forgiveness of that one, and be truly forgiven, not only by God, but by the one you have wronged?"
>
> Sept 7, 1922.

After death we do certainly meet those who have gone on if we have been at all affinitized to them either through love or hate, for these are the two most powerful of all drawing forces and will undoubtedly bring together those who have met on the physical plane. We do have an opportunity to apologize to them for any wrong we have done, but we cannot rectify it upon that plane. We can simply learn its real lessons and understand just how we made the mistake, and in all probability we can make the other one understand it.

But since we make the mistakes on the physical plane we must come back to that plane to rectify them. This physical world is the world of acts and deeds and facts, while the other plane is the plane of thoughts and understanding. In other words, after passing on we look back over our life and we see and understand far more perfectly than while we were on Earth exactly the causes for making mistakes and also how we could have done better. And we also meet those who have been connected with the mistakes and who are also looking back over their Earth-life and are seeing the other side of the mistakes. Thus in a sense there is a mental rectifying of the mistakes because each one is able to see the things from the higher standpoint. And when the time comes you will incarnate near together and the mistakes can be fully rectified.

As to the experience which has caused the mistake you speak of, there is no doubt but that you will meet your husband, for already he is seeking to commune with you. He is very ready to forgive and is prepared to make all right in another life. He is very close to you, and even now, before you pass out, you can sit down quietly and call him by name and in the name of the living Christ say to him that you are sorry for the mistakes you have made; ask his forgiveness, and we are quite sure you will feel he really does forgive you and really does understand.

Therefore it is not wise to think over the affair and let it worry you or upset you. It is over with as far as this first phase is concerned. The present phase is for you to live a life which will truly prove to your husband that you are sorry. Remember he is not gone, but is still very close and he loves you with a love you could never understand. He realizes already that you have seen your error and that you do really love him, because you realize he is your own true mate. Do not strive to forget, but strive to hold his memory close to your heart. Talk to him in the Silence and know that he hears, that he is with you; that because he loves you and sees your sorrow he does not want to pass on, but will wait for you; and that somehow in God's good time the opportunity will be given you to make all right.

> "It was such a comfort to know that my husband is being taken care of. Our boy, who was five in April, saw his father—and it frightened him. A peaceful look came over my husband's face—and I could not believe that he was gone."
> Aug. 4, 1922.

We are glad our letter brought comfort to you. We can tell you that at present your husband is still resting, absolutely sleeping. As you know, it is not wise to disturb such a sleep, even by longing for his presence. We know that you do feel lonesome, but try, when this lonesomeness comes, to send a blessing to him in the name of the living Christ, for although we should not disturb those who are thus resting, yet a blessing sent by one who is here brings to those resting a radiant light and comfort.

Try to give the little boy some idea of the beautiful temple of rest where his father is at present sleeping. Tell him that his father has entered into a beautiful place of rest where he is watched over by loving friends; that a divine radiant Light is around him; that sweet music fills the air and loving angelic beings watch and wait for his complete renewing of life. But tell him that it will be a long time before his father will be able to come back to this Earth; that he himself must grow up to be a man and must always send his father love and blessings, because these blessings become beautiful angelic forces when they reach the higher realms and help to guide his father and keep him from making mistakes.

The peaceful look which came over your husband's face after the choking was over was a recognition of the angelic beings who were waiting to lift him out of this dark world where conditions were so hard to bear and to take him into the place of rest. It was a beautiful passing over, and your simple prayer, "God help him," was the cry of your Soul, but God had already taken care of him and helped him, for it is God's help, whether He sends His angels or whether He sends any other helper. God works through many forces and beings.

> "Regarding a future state of animals I understand there are none. I had been under the impression that when the breath left their bodies, the latter returned to dust while something corresponding to the Soul, conveyed in a finer body, would rest awhile in the astral before returning to earth conditions."
>
> Nov. 10, 1922.

Animals have no individualized Soul and yet each class of animals is a part of and under the guidance of what is called a Group-Soul. It is only when we reach the human stage that one body can express all that the Soul desires to express. In the animal kingdom it takes all the animals of any one species to express the Group-Soul which in itself is a divine outshining. It is the duty of the Group-Soul to guide and prepare the atoms of these creatures to take a more personalized part in the body of a human being during future evolution.

While animals have no Soul they do have an astral body which has its appropriate life in the astral world. For further particulars see our *Realms of the Living Dead*.

Chapter VII

PRAYER

> "Will you be so kind as to send me two sets of prayer cards and tell me just when and how often to use each?"
>
> June 16, 1924.

Each Soul should use the prayer his Inner Self demands at any particular time. That is why we have so many. But we do not expect the pupils to say all of them at any one time. They are all spiritual food and each student has a choice. We might say we set the table and put on this table food for all who come, knowing that each has various tastes and needs.

Moreover these prayers we send out are by no means the only way of asking, but they are samples of how to ask. Very often when we are in great need of help for any special purpose the prayers we say from our own heart, and in our own words are much deeper and have more meaning to us than if we were told to say such and such words. Therefore, altho we like to have the students love the prayers even as we do and to find them expressive of their needs, yet we do not demand it. We say pray to your Father-in-heaven as the Spirit within you gives you utterance. It is well, however, for the student to commit to memory prayers covering various needs so he will have suitable words spring to his lips almost instinctively in time of need.

> "I understand, in a measure, the power of prayer, at least, the prayer of those who are advanced. I also understand to some extent the changes brought about within ourselves through prayer; but I never feel as if I were of real help to others when I pray for them."

Prayer, is sometimes defined as "The soul's sincere desire, uttered or unexpressed." Keep on repeating this to yourself. Think out what it means and if you once grasp it we do not think you will say that you cannot believe in prayer or the power of prayer unless the prayer is offered by those who are advanced. Very often those who are least advanced have the most sincere and earnest desires and those desires, if soul desires, are prayers.

Sincere prayer always reaches to the throne of God. Those who have followed the philosophy of so-called New Thought in its various phases are quite familiar with the wonderful power of thought. Now, prayer is thought with something else added to it, namely, "the Soul's sincere desire," which is more than thought. Therefore try to realize that when you cannot help another by acts or words you can still pray; that by your prayers you are joining yourself in aspiration to the Divine; that you are praying for those things that you feel are the wish and the design of God; hence your prayers cannot fail to be answered, altho they may not always be answered all at once.

> "Sometimes when offering up certain prayers of the Order, I seem overcome with a wave of emotion that nearly blinds me. I have been a self-contained and self-controlled man all my life. I can face war and death, and have done so more than once. I am not emotional. What is the meaning of this experience?"
>
> May 22, 1923.

Your experience is not by any means mere emotionalism, nor is it anything you can at first control, neither is it peculiar to yourself. It is simply that you touch the higher Divine Realms, and whenever a person does this, at once the emotions naturally respond, at first in an almost uncontrollable manner. Yet of course this is one of the things we must ultimately learn to control. In fact, in the little book, *Light on the Path*, this is one of the things alluded to when it says, "Before the eyes can see they must be incapable of tears." This does not mean ordinary tears of emotion or personal grief of any kind, for these are supposed to have been overcome ere we reach the point where those teachings appeal to us. It means that ere we can really become a seer—for remember well we feel before we can see—we must have grown so calm and so accustomed to the vibrations of the Divine Plane that no longer are our eyes blinded with tears.

For your comfort we will say that in the beginning of our work, when Mrs. Curtiss touched this Divine Realm and the Teachings began to be given out, the tears would pour from her eyes in streams, altho she was unconscious of them. They came so copiously that after the lesson her lap would be wet with them, and all this without any consciousness of it and without any emotion. Also Dr. Curtiss, even in his public lectures, when he reached a certain point where his words touched Divine Love and seemed to bring it down to the audience, could at times scarcely control his voice, because of the overwhelming higher forces which caused the apparent emotion. Yet this was not emotionalism, but simply the overwhelming force of Divine Love and the higher consciousness. But continued contact with such high currents of force has long since enabled them to control the seeming emotion.

> "I find praying by word very difficult, and this method seems to me to be accompanied by forced feelings which are not sincere. Is it a sign of spiritual lack?"
>
> Oct 4, 1923.

We are so apt to think we are praying when we are simply indulging in more or less pleasing thoughts. Words are often a necessary part of prayer. Also words are something which has been given to man only, among all of God's creations, therefore they are a gift held back for the highest manifestation of God on earth. Every word we speak and every letter of which the words are made radiates a mighty and marvelous force which helps greatly to carry that which we are seeking for, not only to God Himself, but through every part of the world. For the right kind of words, especially such words as the *Prayer for World Harmony*, vibrate to every part of the Earth and bring about just that which they are intended to bring.

For this reason until you learn first of all to recognize the vital use and vital help of words and until you can think in words and really understand them, it is often helpful to repeat prayers just by word of mouth, even if the words seem to mean nothing to you. Repeat the prayers and while you are thus repeating them have a little period of meditation in which you try to put the words entirely out of your mind and simply seek to let your aspirations and feelings go out, as you say this is most helpful to you. Also, often when we do not feel inclined to pray, if we repeat the words they bring us into the right attitude, hence do us much good.

We need have no fear of the essence of any prayer which has been repeated with all our heart ever being lost. It cannot be lost. For words rightly used can create and re-create. But words wrongly used will bring to man himself a curse, not from God, but the curse of using sacred forces for wrong ends. Remember die *Bible* tells us, "Every idle word that men shall speak they shall give account thereof in the day of judgment," and the day of judgment for you may be tomorrow or at any time in your life.

> "Prayer and faith prevented a terrible operation to me. Now a great blow has fallen. My husband has lost his position because of alcohol and now we are likely to lose our little bungalow. He does not touch drink now and does not even seem to miss it."
>
> June 3, 1922.

Keep on saying the prayers just as you are doing and we will also mention your name and your husband's as we have been doing in our daily services. Try to repeat the *Healing Prayer* and the *Prayer of Protection* each day at noon and realize that you have joined with us and with all our students everywhere in sending out this great protecting living force.

We must, however, explain to you exactly how to make this thing demonstrate. For instance, never pray that you shall have such and such a thing, but simply lay all problems upon the altar, and in perfect faith and confidence know that your prayers have been heard; that the loving Christ wants you to have *the thing which is best* for you; consequently if it is wise and best that the bungalow should rent or be sold, then it will be done. If not, it means that for some reason there is something greater waiting for you and that your loving Father does not want you to be hampered. Rest absolutely in this knowledge of the great love which is leading you in the right way.

> "Sometimes I am frightened at the heights of spiritual ecstasy which seem to prevail within me, and then more frightened at the material depression into which I drop. I cannot make myself pray when I know it will be only mechanical."
>
> July 21, 1922.

As to the spiritual ecstasy which seems to prevail and is then followed by a great depression, that is but the Law of Rhythm and is intended to teach us poise. In other words, when the great ecstacy comes, instead of letting it carry you away completely, remember that on this Earth-plane you will be carried just as far down into the depths as you have permitted yourself to be carried to the heights. Just as on the ocean, if a wave lifts you very high, the trough between it and the next wave will be very deep. So learn to sail the little boat of your personality in such a way that you can remember the ecstasy and the beauty and the love that has uplifted you and can let it temper or neutralize the despondency which tends to follow. Also remember to say: "All things come from the Great Law and I will not be either elated or too much depressed."

As to your idea of not praying unless you feel like it, there again you are permitting yourself to sink down into the trough of the sea, for one of the greatest buoys we can have in the ocean of life is prayer. And if when we feel depressed we force ourselves to say, for instance, the *Prayer for Light*, if we keep on saying it and try hard to believe it, the Light will never fail to come, because we are sending up our highest spiritual power, which will cleave the darkness and let the Light come through. Remember the Christ has said, "I will never leave thee nor forsake thee." When we are on top of the wave in ecstasy we do not need prayer, hence praise takes its place quite naturally. When we have touched the Divine Realization, "We praise Thee, O Lord," comes spontaneously; hence we adore and do not need to pray except a prayer of thanksgiving. But when we are down we need to pray with all our hearts that we may counteract the downward sweep, and not let ourselves say, "There is no use trying."

We never know how to sail our little boat until we have put it to the test. As well might a mariner say, when the storm comes and the boat is rocked by the tempest, "I will do nothing in the way of taking in sail, etc., because there is no use. I am helpless before the wind and the waves." On the contrary, that is the time to work. And when we are down that is the time to pray.

> "Have you any prayers suitable for children?"
> Oct. 18, 1922.

As to prayers for children we would recommend first the *Prayer for Light* and the *Morning Prayer*, also the *Healing Prayer*. You might also add the *Prayer of the Four Angels*: "Four corners to my bed. Four angels round my head, one to watch and one to pray, and two to drive all harm away. Matthew, Mark, Luke and John, bless the bed that I lie on."

Another is the *Prayer of the Three Doors*: "O Lord Christ, open the door of my body to perfect health. O Lord Christ, open the door of my mind to perfect understanding. O Lord Christ, open the door of my heart to perfect spiritual realization."

Chapter VIII

COMMUNICATION AND GUIDANCE

> "Is it possible to communicate with a loved one who has passed from earth life? I have seemed to commune in sleep, but on awakening can remember only a feeling of his love as if I had realized it."
>
> Oct 4, 1923.

There is no doubt but that you can communicate with one who has passed over, but much depends upon the methods used and the condition of the one who has passed over. If one has suffered intensely or was very old he would have to take considerable rest before being able to take up any work whatever, especially anything so difficult and so harrowing at first as communicating with this world.

As to communicating during sleep with one who has passed out, it is quite possible this may have been so, for even tho your loved one might be having a period of rest, yet when you go to sleep you yourself could go to your loved one and communicate through thought power. This would be more a communion of love with the highest and best part of your loved one. Quite naturally you would not be able to bring back anything except the feeling of deep and abiding love, for love would have been the vehicle for your communion.

Communication and Guidance

> "How shall I become successful in communicating with other worlds through the planchette?"
>
> Oct 7, 1923.

In general we do not think it wise to use the planchette, for if any discarnate Soul can influence your hand and make you write, it can also obsess and influence your whole body and mind in the same way. You have the higher Divine Guidance and your effort must be to find that Guidance, or let us say, to correlate with your Divine Self. Do not ask any discarnate entities to help you, for those who are capable of using the planchette are but little more advanced than are you yourself. And as we said before, they are apt to obsess you. We suggest that you study what we say in our *Realms of the Living Dead* as to the dangers of such forms of communication.

> "May I ask that you send me a line or two? Whatever seems best for me according to the Divine Plan. A few lines from the Teacher would be deeply appreciated."
>
> Oct. 10, 1923.

One of the most important of all our teachings is that a pupil is not ready to receive any direct special teaching as to his spiritual needs until they have so filtered into his own consciousness that at least he has a somewhat dim idea of what he wants, to the extent of being able to put it into the form of a question. This is not a mere arbitrary ruling of this Order, but is the very essence of the Divine Plan. The Divine Flame is forever coming down from on high and penetrating into all physical things, especially into the hearts and lives of those who are seeking to follow and unfold within themselves the higher inspiration and wisdom which is contained within the Divine Flame.

The first necessity is that the pupil shall feel this unfoldment and shall study it over quietly and earnestly until it truly begins to unfold within him the wisdom or knowledge of the special thing he desires. When this has been unfolded the pupil can put it into the form of a definite question and send it to the Teacher, not so much for the sake of hearing an unknown mystery declared to him, but rather to hear the confirmation of what the inner Voice has told him. To give a pupil information before he has tried to formulate his needs is like offering food to one who is not hungry.

Therefore, dear student, we must seemingly refuse to unfold to you that for which you ask. But in reality if you accept what we have said and meditate upon it and ask for guidance you will find we have not failed you, but have really given you the answer which is best for you to have at this particular time of your unfoldment.

> "Nearly two years ago we began to write with the planchette. Among those who wrote one calling himself Michael Archangel, giving us instructions of the highest order. Then came a change. One came who called herself Astoreth, or the Devil. Because of this influence, who calls herself the 'Doorkeeper', we have not used the planchette for nearly a year. Can you tell us how to get rid of her?"
>
> Jan. 18, 1923.

If you have carefully read our *Realms of the Living Dead* you will see that we clearly discountenance the use of the Planchette, Ouija Board or any of those physical means of communication. Moreover we say that, altho they often begin with some grandiose name, they very quickly reveal what they are in reality.

As to how to get rid of this entity—and it is the same one who came at the very beginning—we would say, use commonsense; that is, know that no holy or Divine Being would under any circumstances begin by giving himself such absurd names as did this one, for humility is the keynote through which we enter into the Divine Realms. So the first rule is to use commonsense, just as you would about a friend who came to you on the physical plane and declared she was Queen Victoria or the ruler of the world, etc. You would quickly say such a person was a humbug. On the astral plane such an entity is often a vain egotist or perhaps a demon who is seeking to garb himself as an angel of light. The *Bible* has told us plainly. "For Satan himself is transformed into an angel of light." Truly when we meet with such problems, if we would diligently read our *Bible* and see what is said regarding such conditions, nine times out of ten we would get our answer and save ourselves much unhappiness and trouble.

However, the thing has gone to such an extent that it is almost an obsession and there is but one way out of it, namely, to pray earnestly and try to unite your consciousness with the Christ. Say "In the name of the Living Christ I will have nothing to do with you or any entity who needs to communicate through such physical mediums as Planchette, Ouija, etc."

Remember that you yourself must be the doorkeeper. And if you are a faithful doorkeeper, would you open the door to everyone who knocked if you knew you were in a dangerous country where the enemies were waiting to rush in and attack you? No, you would fill your home (your body) with the living force of the Christ, with Divine Love, which is the only thing which can keep out the curiosity which would induce you to open your door to any such condition. But if it had once been opened you would go to this great Love and lay your heart bare before it and cling to it and ask for protection. Kill out all curiosity in regard to all astral matters, knowing that as you love and obey and live in the consciousness of the Christ, all these things will be taken care of.

> "A young man comes to me with a communication which came to him through the automatic writing of a sincere woman who did not believe in Spiritualism. What do you think of the message?"

As to the automatic message, in some parts of the message there seem to be certain truths, yet they seem to be much interwoven with the imagination of the transcriber. He should realize that on the side of life from which communications and prophecies come, especially for other persons, there are certain laws which must be recognized and taken into consideration.

One of the first and most important of these considerations is how to distinguish between a message itself and the quite natural and inevitable interpellation of the imagination of the one delivering it which so commingles with the message itself as to make it only too often a menace rather than a help. This message is undoubtedly such a mixture, that is, it is the sincere effort of one quite untrained—in fact not even experienced—to repeat the first vague whisperings which come to her from the unknown.

Like all such early attempts—and, alas, only too often all future attempts unless the ability to discriminate is gained, the message is filled in and padded out by a vivid imagination into what she thinks it should be. Therefore we advise you to tell the young man that he must follow the universal law applying to all communications from the unseen, namely, to challenge them inwardly with all his heart and ask to be led and guided and protected from all falsehood and misunderstanding.

> "How can I get personal guidance from Mahatma K. H.? I wrote to ....at ....India, to send my enclosed letter to Mahatma K. H. Will your Teacher inform me if the Mahatma received my letter?
>
> June 12, 1922.

As to your desire to come into touch with the Mahatma K.H., in our conception regarding such communications we differ widely from the teachings largely promulgated by the ..... As you have doubtless heard and know, it was given out that after the departure from this Earth of the great Soul, Madame Blavatsky, the Masters had withdrawn and would not come into personal communication with their pupils before the end of this present century, *i.e.*, about 1975. But in spite of this widely circulated report there are many in the ...., especially ...., who claim to come into personal touch with her Masters. Now, from our knowledge what was meant by this report was that the Masters would no longer come into physical every-day touch with Their pupils in the way of answering letters, etc., because in the early days that privilege had been so much abused. As perhaps you know, the foundation of the many inharmonies in the .... (persecution of ....and many other conditions resulting in the inharmony prevailing today) was started in what we would call childish quarrels over supremacy in receiving personal letters from the Masters.[1]

We would have little respect for the Great White Lodge were such a policy continued, yet there is no doubt whatever that the Great Lodge of Masters is still concerned intimately and deeply with the affairs of the world; that They are helping in every way to promulgate the higher ideals of Their Teachings. But

---

[1] See *The Mahatma letters to A.P. Sinnet*.

having found that this intimate physical communication awoke in humanity only rivalry and inharmony. They now work in quite a different way; in fact, in a very impersonal way. Whenever a pupil desires to ask really vital questions, there are certain avenues through which the answers will be sent, but they will be sent in an absolutely impersonal manner, with no name of any special Master signed to them. Every communication given out is given in such a way that there can be no claim of the personality to have had greater privileges than anyone else.

In other words, every communication from the Masters comes for the good of humanity and in a way not to add to the vanity of the individual. Therefore, we would not, if we could, tell you whether the letter you sent to the Headquarters was received by Master K. H. or not. But we will say to you that if you have anything which is absolutely vital and to which you wish to receive an answer, provided you have fulfilled the requirements pointed out in our Letter of Information, we will lay it before the Lodge and take the answer from any source which in the wisdom of the Lodge is considered to be best, without demanding any signatures.

> "Thank you so much for your kind letter regarding my brother. Is it possible for me to know what he has escaped from by his sudden death? It is a great comfort to think things are being made easy for him; the bewilderment must be terrible."
>
> Sept. 20, 1922.

We are glad that it is such a comfort to you to hear that your brother is being taken care of.

As to what he has escaped from, it would be difficult to answer this question. It is certainly known, yet like the lives of all of us whose records are kept in the archives of the higher realms, few are permitted to know or give them out. Sufficient to say that in the wisdom of the great Lord of Life, his fate was a happier one than had he lived. It was not, however, an arbitrary decree that he should pass out in such a seemingly untimely and sudden manner. That was his Karma.

If you know anything of the Law of Karma you will realize that through our past lives and acts we have set up certain causes which must in this life be fulfilled. In his case the results would have been very harrowing and trying, and his endeavor to meet them would have not only brought greater suffering to him, but might also have pushed back his further spiritual development. For he had not been interested in any of these higher teachings and refused to listen, so that he would not have known how to meet such conditions. Also his next incarnation would have been far more difficult than his present one. So, because with this Karma of suffering there were certain noble characteristics, which are just as surely Karma as anything else, and because these noble characteristics could be used by the great Divine Teachers to help to bring about the changes so quickly coming to this globe, it was kindest and wisest to permit him to pass out quickly and see his mistakes.

This he is already doing. Also the higher desires for the betterment of humanity are awakening in him. He always did desire to help humanity, but could not see that to do so he must first help himself by bringing out his better qualities and stifling some of his personal traits. Therefore, on the Other Side of life it will be easy to help him to see not only what is needed, but also what humanity is about to face. He seems almost at once to be responding to the urge to become a helper and to give up not his life but his personal desires and his fixed thoughts so that he may prepare himself to be a worker, a true worker for the Christ.

> "I re-read the Song of Solomon with delight but I must own that certain crudities of expression disturb and jar upon the mind which tries to reach up to the sublimity of the Loved One. Why these coarse blemishes?"
>
> Jan. 4, 1923

As to the disturbance in your mind when trying to assimilate the Song of Solomon, you must understand first just how inspiration is given. If some being, be he great or not, comes to us and personally repeats to us certain things which we write down, then we are not really writing under inspiration, but merely under dictation; sometimes very ordinary guidance from the astral plane, yet at other times very high and beautiful guidance from the higher realms. Occult inspiration results when the great Hierarchy called the Lodge of Masters meet together and, let us say, think out some problem that it is important for humanity to know. Then it is broadcasted telepathically, much as radio is broadcasted on Earth. Everyone who is attuned to the rate of vibration of the idea sent out receives it, yet each one receives it according to his own intellectual unfoldment and explains it in his own language and to the very best of his ability.

Therefore the ones who wrote that wonderful book were certain seers who could reach into the Divine Realm whence that great lesson was sent forth. But living in an early day when all things were expressed in language more or less coarse, they did the best they could, and in their symbols and allegories used more or less coarse comparisons and language. You will find this same thing throughout the *Bible*. But instead of saying, "I do not believe the *Bible* because it is so coarse. I cannot accept it," remember how its different parts have been written; that they are none the less inspired because written in a coarse language; that true inspiration is never given word for word. As we said, only astral control does this, and this is one of the tests which should always be applied.

If we can once get this firmly fixed in our minds, all temptation to disbelief because of different expressions disappears. Human beings have been made in the image of God and must evolve closer and closer to their model. And this is especially true of their Higher Mind, and as they thus climb upward this Higher Mind unfolds more and more perfectly so that they can express this inspirational thought in more beautiful language. But all classes of mankind must be taught, and so the ones who cannot express beautifully are nevertheless doing their duty and expressing the inspiration in the best language they can conceive of. In fact, could we lift our consciousness more closely to Divinity and realize that we also are Divine and one with our Father, we would have no questionings at all, but would know "even as we are known." This will come some time, for it is only man and his disobedience that is holding it back.

Do not take literally or believe in anything which makes God a cruel God, for God is love. God is Love and Love is God. Therefore, it is only His love for this world that can save us all.

Altho the *Bible* is full of Divine Truth, yet we must use the key of our own inner understanding. We must ask for Light, because we must remember that the *Bible* was written down in a time and by a people who did not think as we think. Therefore they interpreted the divine knowledge—which was radioed to them from the Divine—in a way which to this generation sounds indeed horrible in many respects. So in seeking to understand the Bible, take as your key this thought. And the same thing applies to you as an individual, *i.e.*, seek for the Divine, the real, the true, the helpful, the beautiful, and pass over all those things which sound so horrible and which do not appeal to you. In spite of these things which seem horrible, there is so much of marvelous help in the *Bible* that little by little you will find the light of its beauty spreading over all the darkness of man's misunderstanding and man's mistranslation. Remember when we say translation we do not mean the translation of one language into another, but the translation into man's thoughts of God's radiant consciousness and living power.

> "My departed mother started to write through my hand. Since then I have had much help from two Teachers, but I often wonder whether it is right to do it, as I am occasionally told not to write for a while."
>
> May 14, 1923.

Automatic writing can be a snare or it can be a help: all depends on the method and the one who is trying it. Almost always in the beginning it is some teacher or loved one who desires to help you and finds it possible to help in that way.

It is, however, always wise to challenge "In the name of the living Christ; " and to hold the firm idea that you will not be fooled or led astray or flattered into accepting anything but truth. Say a little prayer each time you sit down for automatic writing. Say "Father, preserve me from all falsehood. Put around me the armor of Divine Truth and give me only that which is helpful to me." Thus you can safely trust what comes, and you will find you are receiving much help.

Nevertheless automatic writing is not the highest or the best way to receive teachings, for it is quite possible to receive your teachings telepathicly directly from the Divine Helpers. We advise that you study our books, especially *Realms of the Living Dead*. Study sincerely and earnestly and repeat this same prayer we have given you each time you sit down to study the books or the lessons. Then go on with your automatic writing under these conditions, but realize that when you have reached the point where you can get the teachings in a more direct and higher way then stop your automatic writing.

The great trouble with so many is that when the time comes for their automatic writing to cease they get upset and disturbed and insist on its continuance. But because the higher Teachers have found they are ready to take up some other form of teaching and They no longer give it through the automatic writing, then some other entity is apt to step in who cannot be relied on, who simply flatters their vanity, and who tries to make them believe they are receiving the same high teachings. As we have said, it is always necessary to challenge "In the name of the living Christ."

Inspirational writing differs from *automatic* writing in that the hand of the writer is not *controlled* by the communicating entity, hence this is an *independent* and *constructive* method of communication. In this case the communicator flashes the message into the mind of the writer by telepathy, and the writer consciously and of his or her own volition and free-will puts it down either in the language of the communicator or in the writer's own words. This is the method used by St. John in recording the visions of *Revelation* when the angelic communicator said: "What thou seest, write in a book."[2] Strive until this method supersedes the automatic.

---

[2] 1 *Revelation*, I, 11.

Chapter IX

FINANCIAL PROBLEMS

> "Can you tell me why all my financial efforts seem to be thwarted, no matter how hard I try. Would it be right to pray to God for help, or is He above such sordid matters?"

In this world where for the present at least finance has such an important place, we quite naturally find financial problems difficult to deal with. But there is a most occult reason for this, for through all the ages the financial problems have been thrown aside by the aspiring ones and handed over to what we might call the masses of unenlightened persons. It has been considered a sign of spirituality if we are willing to be poor and miserable and helpless and give over our responsibilities to those who are simply worldly-minded. The world would not be in the condition it is today if all of us had realized that there is no mistake in any of the manifestations of Divinity; that altho finances are not the ultimate force which will rule the world, nevertheless there is a great lesson to be learned from them. Consequently we owe a duty to them, and if from the very beginning everyone who had any amount of financial force brought to him by the Divine Law had taken it as a sacred trust to be used for the uplift and help of the world, we would not find things as they are today; neither would we be so far back in the scale of evolution.

However, as the old saying has it, it is never too late to learn. We must begin at once to realize that the renunciation of worldly wealth, etc., simply means the renunciation of our own personal desire for it in order to gratify our own wishes; that we do, however, still want it as an avenue through which we can strive to uplift and help humanity; that therefore we do expect to have at least some money, and that when we have it we must be tested as to the reality of our promise that we want it only as an avenue of help for the world. We must recognize that personally we are of little influence to the world if we are poor and miserable and hampered. Then we will find that our heavenly Father will give us just as much as He sees we are able to use.

We must begin, therefore, with what we have, be it little or much. If we have much, we will gladly give of that to accomplish the work of the Lord. If we have little we will "do our diligence" gladly to give of that little. And then, like the widow's mite, we will see it always sufficient for our needs, for this is the attitude of mind which money is intended to teach. And as soon as the majority of humanity grasp and understand this, money will have no more place in the unfoldment of the great Law of Life.

> "Will you kindly explain the real cause why in our financial need we seem to be tied hand and foot in our effort to bring in our supply. If it is anything in our personality we shall do our best, with the help of the Father, to transmute it into the desired quality."
>
> April 6, 1922.

Your trouble, which you rightly surmise has its roots in your personality, hence will persist until it is transmuted, is as follows: You are so earnest, sincere and over-sensitive in this physical embodiment that the Great Divine Law—the Law of your Good—had to place you in conditions of a diametrically opposite character from those you have contacted in your previous lives that you might round out your character and put into practice that which you had learned mentally. Hence you find yourself in a most material age and in a country where—looking at it from an inner rather than from an outer viewpoint—the lessons of materiality must be learned and the inner essence of them and their reason for existing must be built into the race consciousness. Naturally this is a most difficult era and a more than difficult lesson for the really advanced Souls to understand and learn. Yet since the One Life must penetrate from the center to the circumference ere the cycle is complete, only when the advanced guard of Souls and the Race itself have truly assimilated all that materiality holds for them can the greater Life Wave make its next turn on the upward cycle.

We are now near the turn, hence, materiality, with its degraded standards and its brutal selfishness, is fighting for its continued supremacy against the force of the life-tide which must inevitably sweep away such old conceptions and standards. But as we round this point in the cycle there is much for the Children of Light to learn and put into practice if they are to be as wise as the Children of the World.

The lesson to learn is, firstly, to be more positive with material conditions and substance; to fully understand that wealth is not a mere negligible incident, something to be despised by the advanced Soul while at the same time it is being ardently desired. It is rather a thing, ephemeral in itself, yet given to this age to uplift and bless. Hence it is not to be scorned or treated lightly or thrown away as so many—you among them—have done in past lives, taking vows of poverty, etc. Such vows were quite easily kept when you were supplied by an institution in which all individuals were taught to have no personal interest in what they should eat or wherewithal they should be clothed, but which comes very hard today when you find the old vows still overlapping yet are confronted with new conditions in which you must support not only yourself but wife and child in the comfort which they have a right to expect.

That old vow will hold until you learn its true inner meaning and fulfill it in spirit and in truth. This inner meaning is *not to despise anything* which the Great Law brings to us, for nothing can pass away from mankind until it has been blessed by man through his using it for the highest good, which in this case is to help to change the common idea of the orthodox world that wealth is only a temptation to the advanced Soul and can be enjoyed only by those who have chosen to live for worldly pleasures, instead of looking upon wealth as a thing to be used for the highest good of all.

The true mystic's "vow of poverty" means that we will take or even want nothing selfishly for ourselves alone, but that we recognize the tremendous force of wealth and, because it has heretofore been used to degrade mankind, its control must now be taken from those who have thus degraded it and used by the spiritually enlightened to uplift it. It is therefore the duty of all advanced Souls to secure as much as possible in a legitimate way, and they will obtain it exactly in proportion as they prove by their lives that they can use it to bless and uplift. The Father knows that those thus enlightened must have their physical wants supplied and He will attend to it and help them to get as much as they show themselves capable of using wisely and constructively for the good of all.

The whole old medieval ideal of institutions, brotherhoods, orders, etc., which fed and clothed their members and took all personal responsibility for worldly conditions of prosperity from them was a perverse understanding of a Divine Truth. God will provide, not only the necessities of life, but a bountiful supply for our needs, just as the old monkish Orders did, but the individuals in His service must do their part; must prove their ability to attain it honestly and to use it wisely. He will guide them if they ask and follow, but will not give it to them without an effort on their part. In your particular case we advise you to be more positive with financial and physical conditions and to see to it that justice is done.

> "At one time, thru my use of a strong mental development, I could keep well, demonstrate financial success and all went well with me. But about three years ago my business failed me, then my health and now, altho living a true life and praying and using all my mental powers, which are as strong as ever, I cannot demonstrate anything. Can you help me?"
> July 19, 1923.

You have, as you say, made great demonstrations through . . . ., which is a mental philosophy in which the mind and the brain and the power of thinking are the main factors. Therefore, because you are at this time earnestly seeking for a higher and deeper understanding and are sincerely asking to be set right, you have reached a point where it is imperative that you learn the divine inner understanding of Truth. This is, that the mind is at best but an instrument of the human personality, using the brain as its physical organ, and by the power of thought capable of using this great instrument either as a means of communication—through the Higher Mind—with the higher Divine World, or by using only the lower mind, merely as a promoter and leader of the human side of life. The demonstrations you say you have made are easily explained when you understand the mighty power of the mind, which can of its own power shape and force circumstances and bring about results which seem to the ordinary person quite marvelous.

But, dear student, you must now take a step higher. You must realize that this mind of yours can shape not only the thoughts that rule your personality, but it can also unite you with the divine side of life; can awaken within you that mysterious Divinity which is ruler of all things. But ere this marvelous Divine Awakening can take place, all that you have heretofore depended on in the form, let us say, of mental magic, must be swept away. You must find out that it can no more rule your life; that in spite of the wonderful demonstrations you were capable of making, there is something wrong, something you cannot conquer. Therefore, our advice is to think over carefully, logically and prayerfully what we are saying and see if you can realize that there is within you a Divine Something that is an outshining of the Godhead; Something that can and will help you first of all to sweep away the hampering conditions, not merely of your life and of your inability to demonstrate wealth, etc., but the greatest of all hampering conditions, *i.e.*, the erroneous belief that the mind is infinitely powerful and that, because it is cultivated and brought to a high state of development, this mind which you call Divine can bring to you just what you need. Between what is known as the lower mind—that which deals with your life on earth—and your Higher Mind, which is capable of union with God, a great gulf is fixed, and only when, by the help of God, you lift the lower mind over this gulf can you use mind for its highest ends.

You will suffer the lack of these things until you learn this great lesson. But once you drop all these ideas and cry out, "O Christ, the Divine Power within me, help me to unfold and develop the great love-force, and the great understanding that back of the mind and back of all life there is a Divine Something which can accomplish that which nothing mundane can touch." Then dropping all preconceived ideas, begin as a little child to learn that which we call Divine Wisdom, which you must learn step by step.

The first step is to come to a realization of this Divinity within and of the inadequacy of mental faculties alone, and to promote and control its development. Then you must begin to realize that the mental power that is given you is but a gift from this Divine Self to be used, not to bring you merely physical things such as wealth, etc., but to bring you into rapport with your Higher or Spiritual Self, and with the Creator of all things. Then you will say, "Not my will but Thine be done," which means that you will make all outer things secondary. You will say, "Let me learn my lesson. I know that my heavenly Father will take care of me and will bring to me whatever is necessary, even tho I have to pass through more or less poverty and conditions which seem to be harrowing and discouraging. Yet ultimately I will emerge into the light of Divine Truth."

This is the first lesson. And when you have learned it or at least realized it and said, "I know this is my lesson," then you will have help to go on putting it into practice. Make the mind an obedient servant of the Divine Self, instead of placing it upon a pedestal to be worshipped.

> "We have both been working in an orthodox church, but sometimes question whether we are doing the best we can. Speaking from a material standpoint we have not been very successful, and we wonder if it is because we are not 'living the life' as we should. We are willing to work for the

kingdom if the Father wants as to and will show us, but we cannot seem to find the answer."
                    Dec. 7, 1922.

We sincerely hope that wherever you are working, whether in the ....orthodox church, in the Society or elsewhere, you will find many opportunities to drop the seeds of Truth, wisdom, love and simplicity, for these are the things most needed at the present time to bring to the world a knowledge of the necessity of co-operation in all fields. Moreover we hope you will spread the *Prayer for World Harmony*, sent you with a previous lesson. Spread it just as widely as possible, for this is more important at the present time than any of you can realize.

As to your failure in financial conditions, there are many reasons for this. One is that it is not so much that you have not been living the right life, but that perhaps you have not had the right comprehension of the financial question. Again, it may be Karma; but back of the lack of finances for many at this particular time there is a universal reason, namely, that we are facing very strenuous upheavals in the industrial, social and political life of the whole planet, very similar to that which has taken place in Russia. And for this reason the Masters feel reluctant in regard to putting forth any great amount of wealth, as it may either be confiscated to make war and to bring about conditions even more dreadful than at present; or if in the possession of those who have higher ideals it may be a cause for their persecution. Thus it will be taken from them and will bring greater misery than a little shortage just now would do.

> "Church attendance seems to be slipping in our family . . . . when they came around for a renewal of our subscription I told them that in view of our other charities and contributions, and the further fact that I could not support their *literal* and materialistic interpretations, our contributions would be cut one-half. As a whole the Church is a good institution and I am willing to do my bit to support it, but not to the detriment of other and more advanced and to me more helpful avenues of spiritual teaching."
>
> Dec. 30, 1922.

We wish to say "Well done." For why should we support that which we do not find helpful, or believe in? especially in these days of clearing up the old conditions and preparing for the new; when every faculty and every condition is needed to make it possible for those we truly believe are seeking to prepare for this great closing up of the cycle and this preparation for the new, to have the power to do so. To be perfectly frank with you, dear student, we believe that if you thought less of your own lack of ability and success and were a little more positive about where you go and where you give the support of your presence and character and money, and studied a little more positively how you could be of the greatest help toward preparing the world for this great change, you would find yourself a greater success than you imagine; a greater business success and hence with more money at your disposal. Do not permit yourself to be swayed too much by circumstances or even by family conditions, still less by a kind of moral laziness which would rather do what the world approved of than take a stand for what you felt to be right.

In these days of testing we know absolutely that the Great Masters are doing all they can—for special reasons—to hold back any large quantity of money from all their particular students who could use it—if they used their brains while doing so—for the great work of helping the world; who should know enough to use it for the best purposes. It is bad enough for those who are more or less drifting with the tide to have money to destroy themselves with, but those who should know better are being kept from this great temptation and are being forced to learn their lesson. Therefore, not only from a spiritual standpoint but from a physical, we know that when you have learned this great lesson and have fully decided where you think your money can do the most good to help push back the evil so overwhelmingly accumulating in humanity, then you will be permitted to have more of it. For once having chosen to devote ourselves to this great work we are given just as much or as little as the Great Law thinks we will use to the best advantage. We have to prove ourselves.

> "I was wishing so much that I had some money that I might begin to pay up my arrears with you, and I found that my daughter to whom I had given the last lesson had tucked a dollar in its folds. We both appreciate the lessons beyond words to tell."
> July 28, 1922.

Your experience as to your wish for money was a decided corroboration of the way real prayers are answered when it is right that we should have the thing we wish for. We appreciate both your desire and your daughter's to help, for after all, altho money is very badly needed, nevertheless it is this honest, sincere and determined desire to do the best you can that truly helps us.

Try to get the idea that if you are poor and hampered for money, it is probably a karmic condition. There are people who in past lives have thrown money away and have accepted voluntary poverty thinking that money was but a snare and delusion. But in this life they find themselves badly needing this very "snare and delusion" and yet are without it. You must realize that your heavenly Father wants you to have whatever is best and necessary for your *spiritual* growth, and that the moment you learn the lesson, *i.e.*, how to take care of it, and that you believe and trust that enough will be given you to get along with, then you will begin to find things coming to you. Do not say, "I do not want money." Do not say, "I will accept poverty if it is my Father's will." It is not your Father's will. If you have poverty now it is because some time in the past it has been your own will.

In reality we will never straighten out the world's ideas of money until we awaken to the fact that money is a necessary instrument for good at the present time and that our heavenly Father wants us to be provided for. Then have trust. Do not expect it to shower upon you all at once, but do expect and pray for and determine that every want which is a real want will be supplied, even as this want that you had for helping the Order was supplied, provided you awaken to your responsibility and do your part.

> "I long to have thousands of dollars that I can give to your great work, but no matter how hard I strive only bad luck, disappointment and ill health ever come to me. I am a true Christian and did give to churches and poor people, but nevertheless I am broke."
>
> March 16, 1923.

We recognize your great desire to give, as you say, thousands of dollars to help on the work of this Order, but are unable to do so. However, the best way to help promote your interests is to pray earnestly and sincerely that it may be possible for you to have something which you can give to the Order. For when we unselfishly pray for someone else, and especially for some good cause, surely this prayer cannot be fulfilled unless we have also enough for our immediate and reasonable needs, for they should be supplied. Therefore the Founders will in turn hold you in the Light that your wants may be supplied, but you with all your heart must pray the same prayer, *i.e.,* that you may have enough to live on and also to help the Order.

By all means shut out of your consciousness the thought of bad luck, etc. As long as we hold fast to the thought that all we can expect are the things you describe, then that is all we ever will get. For we have thus made a law for ourselves that this is our portion; and altho the world is ruled by God Almighty, who is Love, and who desires His children to receive all that is good and necessary, yet the instant man (for man is made in God's image and has the power to create through thought) makes a hard and fast rule that certain things and only such things are coming to him, then such things must come to him until he learns his mistake, because they come through the power of his thought. They are created not by God, or sent by God, but are created in the world by all the people who have corresponding thoughts. And by repeating such words and thinking such thoughts we absolutely make an avenue through which they come to us. There is no such thing as either bad or good luck; we get that which is our karmic due or that which we create and draw to ourselves.

Therefore change these words and instead of saying that nothing but such things shall come to you, say "I know my Father wants me to do a certain work for humanity through the *Order of Christian Mystics,* and if I do my duty and believe that I am going to be able to do this, then He will give me that which is best. My own can come to me only through His great love and His great power. So I will not have my life ruled by the evil things created by man, but will go direct to my Father-in-heaven and receive my heritage."

> "You say that if one is in financial troubles to let you know and you will help. Mine are in the direst muddle . . . . I seem to be stopped dead with my violin as soon as I am in a fair way with getting in pupils. Am I not meant to go on with my violin?"
>
> March 9, 1923.

We are always ready to help our students in all the vicissitudes of life, but when we say we will help them financially we do not mean that we have funds to offer them. Indeed, there is no one who needs financial aid more than do we ourselves because of the many needs of the work. What we mean is that we will advise them and hold them in our prayers that all things necessary shall be supplied, be it financial or any other need which will help them to progress. We ourselves never have had what you would call ample financial supply, yet we always have just enough and every vital want is supplied. And this is what we ask for all the pupils, yet the pupils must have faith, must do the asking and the praying, not to us but to the Father-in-heaven; they must truly believe that when a great need arises somehow the want will be supplied. But they must also work.

If we read the *Bible* carefully we shall find it is full of this idea of work. In one place it says, "Unless ye work neither shall ye eat." Another saying is, "Seek and ye shall find, ask and it shall be given unto you," etc. Therefore all we can do is to encourage you in seeking and asking, by adding our prayers to yours, knowing well that this method is true because we have proved it. For we have never been told we shall have great wealth or great supply except as the great demand for helping humanity arises and we have proved ourselves able to use it.

If, as you say, you are always stopped dead when you think you are making a living with your violin then go into the Silence and ask to be shown definitely whether you have sufficient talent for the violin to depend upon it to bring you in supply, or if there is something else the Great Law desires you to take up. Often we are apt to love a thing very dearly and think it is our great talent, our great source of income, and yet find it is not. Our greatest talents, especially if they be any kind of art, are seldom our best way to make a living; for there is nothing so difficult as to be obliged to subjugate the beloved talent to a worldly standard and make a living by it. We cannot tell you whether you are meant to go on with your violin or not, but if you ask earnestly for guidance the Lord of Life, who is your Divine Friend, who is always with you and eager to help you, will show you in some way which you will recognize at once that it either is or is not your vocation. Remember we are told that if we ask earnestly and prayerfully we shall always be answered. The answer does not always come in words, but it does come in events. When we know we have asked earnestly we shall have no difficulty in knowing beyond a doubt that we have been heard and are being answered.

> "I am having a very hard test, for my worldly duties are most distasteful and seem to crowd out all things that I so long to devote my life to."
> Jan. 9, 1923.

As to the reason of your difficulty, it is a very obvious one, for in your last life you were almost completely shielded from the world. And one of the great faults of the early teaching was that the world was a thing with which those who belonged to any sacred

Order should have no fellowship. This is in reality the great Karma we are all now meeting every one of us, because it had been instilled in us that we were something different from those who remain in the world and do their duty there. Now we must learn that we are not something different; that the world with all its legitimate wants and desires is not something to be shunned; that if we have had the great happiness to be taught something a little higher, then in return it is our duty to help to spread these beautiful ideas, altho this does not always come as easily as it should. However, times change and we must learn to change with them. No matter how difficult it seems we must at least make the effort.

There are many who feel lost when outside the mighty protective wall which was purposely put around all who were willing to come out of the world and, as the *Bible* says, be separate. This, however, is meant to be taken symbolically, for we should be in the world, but not of it. Yet many are reaching a point where they must be helped. Therefore we want you to try to overcome this deadness you feel, this shutting of the door when talking to those who are not your comrades. However, do not learn it too thoroughly. This may sound absurd, but what we mean is do not learn to take down all the barriers; simply ask of the Divine that you may have wisdom to speak and also wisdom to keep silent when it is necessary.

You have been an inmate of certain religious retreats for not only one but several incarnations and have always been very devoted. This does not mean you have reached a point of perfection; far from it, but it does mean you have learned a great deal, and especially to love that which tends toward the mystic, the ideal and the devotional side of life. Having learned this, you must now go back into the world and learn how to put your knowledge into practice. And yet when you count it all up you will find that you have been wonderfully blessed in those who have been brought to you as loving friends with whom you can converse, and also in those who need your help.

> "Is it legitimate and right to make great profits from investments? A man invested $5,000 with . . . . twenty years ago and has since received $18,000,000 for it. Being of the tribe of workingmen I would like every such one to get the full measure of his deserts, consistent with wisdom. Are not enormous profits taking undue toll of the workers who produce the goods?"
> July 18, 1923.

As to the legitimacy of making great profits through investments, such as are frequently made these days, we would say it is by no means legitimate for anyone to make enormous profits. . . .

As to the man who invested five thousand dollars and in twenty years received eighteen millions, this is again simply the working out of a misconceived idea of just profits. The truth is that there should be a real true brotherly understanding that every man, be he rich or poor, has a destiny to fulfill and a great duty toward all humanity. And if he finds his business bringing in such enormous profits, he should prayerfully ask those on the higher side of life just how he could make these profits do the most good, not only for the few who are working for him or who have invested in his business, but for the great mass of humanity, especially for the spread of spiritual Truth. There are many ways this could be accomplished; one step would be to make a better product and sell it at a lower price, or in some way introduce a scheme which would benefit the whole world.

As to your second question, the workingman should indeed get the full amount of his deserts consistent with wisdom. The last part of that sentence contains all the answer, "consistent with wisdom." The workingman is just as necessarily designed to find wisdom and to put it into practice as is the millionaire, indeed in most cases far more, because more simple, more industrious and not so much tempted by the handling of large sums. Truly very often the millionaire finds his wealth like a millstone pulling him down into the depths of unwisdom. However, the workingman is not entirely free from this unwisdom. He must seek for his deserts and will receive them not according to how hard he works or how much he talks or condemns others who have more money than he has, but according to how he tries to live the higher life and to spread this thought that it is not money that is the king of the world, but Divine Wisdom which will help all who seek it for the benefit of the race.

Of course, such enormous profits as you mention are taking toll of the worker, yet they are taking far greater toll of the whole world, workers and all. In fact the workers have a much better chance—because they are workers—of reaching the higher ideals of life, if they will but learn the great lesson. As time goes on, and it is approaching rapidly, there will be a great outpouring upon this poor money-ruled world of the realization of the inability of mere money to bring happiness or lasting good. And it is then that the workingman who has the ability to recognize his duty and to do the best he can will help lift the whole world one step higher, *i.e.*, to think of co-operation and that the worth of a thing is what it can accomplish for humanity, not what it costs.

If we try to follow the Bolshevist doctrine that not only the man of money but also the man of education must be annihilated; that only ignorance can be king and the one who works with his hands be the only accepted factor in the world, then we are tearing down. We must recognize that we need the moneyed man, the educated man and also the working man: above all, the educated man if he is willing to let his brain be illumined by the Divine Light. Therefore the greatest good we can do for humanity is to educate it. God forbid that there ever comes to this country the necessity of passing through this awful change until we have had the means of helping to educate at least enough of our fellowmen to recognize this true principle of co-operation. And this is what we must accomplish, and everyone who is studying and trying to do his best is a helper toward this great work of cooperation. It is not the killing out of any class, but education and co-operation of all that should be our watchwords: the education that depends for its blessing and ultimate success on the inspiration of the Divine.

> "Lately I seem to labor under a severe lack of means. For fifteen years I made no charge for services and I still stand there, except that I want more now to give and to help the work in general."
> Sept. 20, 1922.

Altho it is very beautiful and ideal to make no charge for your services, and altho we have always worked on that principle ourselves, yet we have learned from experience that we have no right to foster in the minds of students the idea that they have no responsibility in helping to support such work. For if they take no responsibility for it they get really very little good out of it. But, as we say, the money must come as a love offering. Otherwise it is not acceptable nor will it truly help the work. So there is an important distinction between charging for spiritual teachings—for this would be compelling students to pay whether they wanted to or not—and asking them to give a free-will offering.

You must see to it that the teachings you give are of such a character as will awaken in their hearts a desire to be a part of the work, or to give that which they can give to support it. It is only one here and there who is capable of properly reaching into the higher realms and receiving and giving out the necessary spiritual teachings, but everyone can give a little of his means to help to support such teachings. For if those who are devoting their lives to helping others have to divide their time between working for a living in ordinary earthly conditions, they find it almost impossible to give the very best in them to the greater work. We tell you all this because we see that you are trying to do the Master's work and we feel that you should know on what lines to work.

It is not simply that we lay down lines of force by giving of our best, but according to our teachings we must try to comprehend that spiritual truth is more valuable than money because more difficult of attainment; that only as we have the financial help of those who truly need this spiritual teaching can our minds be free to reach up and take from the Divine so that we may give freely. There is also a vital truth in the words, "As ye give so shall ye receive." In other words only as we give of that which is given to us—be it money, time or spiritual teaching—in love and humility and with a great desire to be a co-worker with the Masters of Wisdom, will we receive in return from the same great supply that which is needed for our personal support. However, we have found that the mass of humanity needs much enlightenment on this subject before they are willing to recognize the true comparative values of worldly wealth and spiritual enlightenment.

"Must I give up all things for the higher life?"
April 14, 1923.

The Lord Christ does not ask you to give up all worldly things. On the contrary, remember that God Himself created all things and placed you in the midst of them, giving you just the conditions in life which were best for you. Therefore He can judge better than you. Use all that comes into your life not merely for your own selfish gratification, but for the glory of God. If you have money, try to use your highest intuition and give as much as possible to the great work of helping mankind. And it is only when His children deliberately refuse His gifts and will not obey that they have to pass through troubles and trials until they learn to do better.

If a person throws God's gifts back in His face and teaches others to do so, or that God gave us these things only to test us and tempt us, imagine the sorrow that must be felt by a Divine Being who has done so much to make the world beautiful and to bless His children, when He finds them ungrateful and unwilling to take His joys; when they are deliberately tormenting themselves and opening the door to the devils of evil and letting them come in to obsess them.

You see, the main thing is to have good commonsense. And if God is Love, we must learn love—not the ordinary physical love, but what it means to understand Divine Love—to be willing to give, to enjoy and to bless everything we touch.

Chapter X

REINCARNATION

"Why does the Ego in some cases choose a life in which honors and riches enter profusely but unjustly, without any personal effort?"
June 15, 1923.

As to the earth-path that an Ego chooses in any special incarnation, this is largely ruled by the Karma of the individual. For remember the Soul must learn all lessons. It must learn lessons of suffering, sorrow and poverty or even the much more difficult lesson of the proper use of riches, worldly elevation and world adoration and admiration and the pride which goes with it. This is looked upon by "those who know" as a far greater karmic condition to be overcome and a harder lesson to be learned than poverty. When a person is thrust into such worldly honors unjustly it is nevertheless Karma which has earned him the place, not as a reward but really as a great test. The fact that such a person rises to the position is simply one more test to the Ego.

In the path of the Ego's evolution it is said we have three mounts to climb; the first is always one of worldly preferment; then we go down into the valley where all such things are taken from us except the lessons we have learned; then we climb the mental height and again are plunged into the valley, or have great mental ability yet lack all opportunity to study; until finally with all these lessons impressed upon us we laboriously climb the spiritual height.

Whatever place in life an Ego has filled, if it has filled it honorably and learned the lessons out of it, whether that position be high or low, then that Ego has accomplished a great deal, even if the position has been thrust upon it. But we must remember that those things which we have truly learned and impressed permanently upon our higher consciousness are the only things we carry away with us; we are just what our Soul has built into character, not what might be considered our just due from a worldly point of view.

> "Will you kindly give me the teachings of the Order on the following: Shall we again see and know the members of our family and the friends we have loved in this life? If so, how does reincarnation affect it? Are the people we live with the same or some of the same in each incarnation and do we know them as such between incarnations?"
>
> Oct. 11, 1922.

We do teach that after death we meet those whom we have loved and known and been associated with in this life. Yet no matter if they have belonged to our family or circle of friends, if we do not really love, hate or affinitize with them, we leave them. After death everyone enters into the magnetic sphere which agrees with his own special affinitization.

As to reincarnation affecting this, it cannot possibly do so, for very few reincarnate for at least a period of from one hundred and fifty to five hundred years, and frequently the period is much longer, hence have plenty of time to wait for and greet those they have left behind. Often the people we find ourselves associated with in the next incarnation are the same as in this life, especially if we have made any great Karma with them in the past, either through hatred or through love, for friends, families and larger groups generally tend to incarnate together. Yet this is not always so, for sometimes we make Karma with those who are perfect strangers; consequently we must be associated with them until we work out that Karma. However, always between incarnations we find and know those whom we have loved, for love is a quality which brings all together and helps them to understand and thus build into their next Earth-life this mighty power of love. The greatest magnet is love and next most powerful is hate.

> "Why do some occult books teach reincarnation while others deny it? Both quoting teachings from the other side of the veil as their authority."
> April 7, 1923.

This is because some occult books are inspired by those who know the Truth, while others are simply the outgrowth of religious or philosophical thought and are purely personal speculations, or at least written by those who are untrained in any comprehensive philosophy and have never touched the higher truths. Since after passing out we gravitate to those of similar ideas and vibrations, one who knew nothing of reincarnation or who refused to study it here, after passing out would not be likely to meet those who understood it over there, hence would report adversely when communicating. Therefore, the necessity of taking our philosophy from those who really know, and not think that the mere passing out of the physical into the astral gives unlimited understanding.

> "What, when and where was my last incarnation, and when and where will be my next? How long will my present incarnation endure?"
> Oct. 3, 1923.

As to when and where your last incarnation took place, this is a question we are not permitted to answer. Only as the student reaches a critical point where the knowledge of certain events of the past is absolutely necessary for his progress are they revealed to him.

Whenever anyone is told of his past incarnation it is one of the greatest tests his Soul can pass through, hence it is a great mercy that we do not know our past lives. This also answers your second question, namely, as to when and where will be your next reincarnation, for of course your next one will depend absolutely upon your present one; that is, as to how much of the higher divine understanding you are able to build into your physical life and thus register it in your higher consciousness. For while your Divine Higher Self knows all your incarnations, you cannot know them and remember them until you have so demonstrated the divine inner forces that they will be registered on your brain consciousness. Therefore be very careful how you accept either your own imaginings or the sayings of others on this subject.

As to how long your present incarnation will continue, it will continue until you have either accomplished enough to give you a foundation on which to build your next incarnation, or have failed utterly to learn the lessons given you to learn. And no one can tell you what these lessons are except your own inner Divine Self. The way to answer all these questions is to try to correlate your mind with your Higher Divine Self and to ask of this Divine Self that it shall help you to learn the lessons step by step as they come up in your life and that as you accomplish and overcome you may recognize what you have accomplished.

The fact that you feel such a strong desire to read philosophy and religious books and to come in contact with saints means that this is the one thing your past incarnation has succeeded in building into your consciousness. It therefore comes to you as a definite thought and desire in this life.

> "Since I was fourteen years old I have always felt a strong attraction for college men. I seem to have a natural love for men, but I am not attracted to women. Can you explain this?"
>
> May 16, 1922.

Your great trouble is that you are in reality a feminine Soul in a masculine body in this incarnation, and as this is your first incarnation in such a body all your memories and loves, etc., are feminine, *i.e.*, for men rather than for women, it is a difficult condition to work through. That is what causes the great sadness. The way to conquer this sadness is to face the situation and to say to yourself, "All Souls must some time in their evolution learn the opposite side of the sex question. Perhaps I was too exclusively wrapped up in the feminine side and tended to despise or refused to look into or to understand the other side, *i.e.*, the masculine. Consequently I am here in this masculine body that I may learn the lessons of masculinity." Realize it is only a temporary condition and determine to gather all the lessons to be learned, and put your whole heart in it.

Instead of letting your heart go out with such yearning love, or seeking for understanding and sympathy from men, which would be perfectly natural were you in a feminine body, say to yourself, "This is not my new lesson, for I learned that lesson in my past lives. I am now in a masculine body to learn the other side." So try to see the same higher truths as expressed in the better class of women. Try to find in women the education and the mental capacity you so admire in college men. Refuse to be carried away with the mere surface femininity or the kind of women who make light of the real things of life, for in very truth this was the mistake which you yourself made in the past and is the reason why you have to learn this lesson of masculinity now in this life. Try your very best to look at life through the masculine lens. Study it up. You can do this much more completely than we can tell you.

Try to think just what it is you admire in men and say to yourself that you will express those things yourself. Then you will attract to yourself only the advanced women who will be able to appreciate this higher development. You look to others to bring you joy and you forget that you are here in a masculine body, with a complete realization of the sort of men most desirable, yet with the old tendencies to be merely an undeveloped or, let us say, an uninformed woman. Say to yourself, "This is my great opportunity. I will study; I will read and cultivate my intellect and try to make myself a man of the higher class in all that it means. I will not bother my head at all about results, or as to whether I am sought after and loved or not. But I will set to work to be really the thing which I admire." And long before you have accomplished the result you will find these men for whose companionship you so long, seeing in you the desirable traits which appeal to them, and you will also find that you are attracting to you the higher and better class of women.

> "What would be the explanation of abortion, also of death in early infancy and childhood?"
> Oct. 9, 1923.

As to abortion, or death in infancy, there are many reasons for it. In deliberate abortion the great crime is that the Soul is prevented from taking possession of the body and consequently its incarnation is prevented and the mother must bear the Karma. In many cases spontaneous abortion occurs because a number of Souls of very unadvanced development are fighting for possession of the body. This creates such a reaction upon the mother that the result is abortion or premature birth or still-birth. There are also many reasons for death in infancy and early childhood. Often this is caused by the fact that the Soul did not have to incarnate at that time, but came either through a great longing of the mother or the desire of the incarnating Soul to comfort her; or perhaps it was an opportunity to make a touch with the Earth so as to lift the mother's thoughts up to the higher realms. We know of several such cases; for often a worldly mother is led to think of higher things to which she formerly gave but little thought if she has lost a little baby, and she often feels that she can still contact it after it has passed on.

However, you can rest assured that nothing unnatural, even if unusual, can ever happen. Try to remember the difference between the physical and the immortal part of us; that the physical body is made up of earthly substances as a physical dwelling place for an immortal Soul that is Divine and comes from God. Realize that the Soul does not take definite possession of this house of clay until at least the stage of "quickening" is reached, at which time the Soul makes the second faint contact, the first being at the time of conception. There is a more positive contact at the time of birth and then little by little the contact becomes stronger until the child reaches the age of twelve when the incarnating Ego takes full possession of the body, as evidenced by the onset of puberty. It is remembering this fact and making the difference between the mere body of clay, which is only intended as a house for the Soul, and the immortal Soul itself, which will help you to answer such questions as this for yourself.

An immortal Soul does the best it can to find the best body possible, yet there are many undeveloped

Souls who have made such Karma on Earth that it is impossible for them to build up or inhabit perfect bodies. And at every birth there is, we might say, a number of Souls seeking to take possession of each body being prepared. This is especially so after a great war when so many have been thrown out of incarnation while in the full tide of life.

As a general thing the Ego comes to a family to which it spiritually belongs, unless it has made a very definite Karma with some other family to which it does not truly belong. Often a Soul desires to help some family which is less advanced in understanding or spiritual unfoldment and so deliberately makes the great sacrifice of incarnating in such a family. There are innumerable reasons for incarnations, and really the more advanced the Soul the more apt it is to incarnate in seemingly undesirable families or conditions. Therefore, it is not always well to decide that the conditions the Soul meets after incarnating are all the result of its own Karma; for when a Soul has advanced to a stage where it desires to help on the great work of spiritualizing and uplifting the world it may deliberately choose to work sometimes under most difficult and undesirable conditions so that it may bring forth a better understanding of life in those conditions.

Generally when a Soul does this it needs the lessons, or let us say the experiences, because it has reached a point where its sole desire is to pass through difficult experiences for the purpose of helping. But it forgets or perhaps has not yet learned that it is not always the most difficult things that teach us the greatest lessons, for sometimes it is the still, small voice of love and understanding which teaches us the most, yet we often feel it is necessary to pass through the fire and the tempest in order to learn.

If an incarnating Ego has chosen a special family and a special mother to incarnate through and for some reason the foetus does not come to full maturity or dies, the Ego must take another, the next best it can find. This is also one reason why so many advanced Souls find themselves in the wrong places, because having given up the heavenly home and descended into the Earth atmosphere, the Ego cannot go back; it must incarnate, and consequently chooses the next best mother. It is not the laws of Karma which interfere in these conditions, for you must realize that man has been given a certain amount of freewill. In Genesis we are told that after the Earth was made God said to man: "Be ye fruitful and multiply." And again after man was turned out of Eden he was told to till the earth and bring forth fruits of the earth; also bodies for Souls to incarnate in. So parents have the control of such things and if they choose to prevent incarnation they can do so, but they must take the consequences, just as when they refused to plant the fruits of the earth they will find they must starve because they had destroyed the possibility of the growth of the life-giving food which was necessary.

Another karmic reason is that in past ages thousands of persons retired into religious retreats and so refused to give incarnation to the Souls for whom they should have been the parents. When such persons desire to incarnate in this life they must learn what it means to be refused an opportunity to incarnate, either by abortion or through some false ideal of the marriage relation on the part of otherwise advanced parents to whom such Souls are karmicly attracted. If the more spiritually advanced persons refuse to become parents then they are preventing advanced Souls—spiritual teachers, artists, musicians, leaders of thought, etc.—from incarnating at the very time when such are most needed to usher in the new civilization, except such Souls as are willing to incarnate through less advanced parents and in less helpful conditions.

If a child passes out while young it does grow while it is in the higher world until it reaches its normal size, that is, its full stage of Soul-growth; whatever stage of maturity it has attained, yet it never grows old.

Under certain conditions it is possible for Souls who have met an early death, as did so many of the boys in the war, to incarnate immediately and come back and finish out the life thus cut short, often through the same physical parents. This is especially true if such a person had a great work to do for humanity. You must remember we can never possibly work out, as you call it, our physical Karma or our physical life on any other plane than the physical. Yet we have a life to live on all the planes and it is only the life and the lessons we have to learn in the astral and in the higher realms which are continued after death.

> "I should like to feel a little more clear with regard to what is meant or known as 'the spiritual marriage'. I had a dream about it and passed through a ceremony very much like that called taking the veil."
>
> August 5, 1922.

That which is meant by the spiritual marriage is the joining of the lower self to the Divine or Higher Self. But this union only comes after many, many incarnations and tests and experiences.

Your dream was, we believe, but an idealized memory of that which happened to you in a past incarnation. In a past incarnation you were a very sincere and earnest nun and the ceremony of taking the veil is literally a symbol of this higher and greater joining of the lower personality to the Divine. Consequently it was spoken of as a spiritual marriage, or the marriage of the nun to the church.

Chapter XI

THE SEX PROBLEM

> "I have great difficulty in killing out the temptations of sex. Is not the sex problem the great temptation to be overcome ere man can truly gain mastery?"
>
> March 20, 1923.

Regarding the unhappiness of your marital relations, there are many suffering just as you are, mistaking sex desire for love. And so many of these mistakes could have been avoided if the truth regarding marriage and the sex relations were taught. Yet so many of the occult societies, which should be leaders in these teachings, either do not understand, or they avoid this subject.

Firstly, we should have a better understanding of what marriage is and why there is such an almost irresistible effort by all mankind to seek for happiness in the marriage state. We must realize that marriage is an expression on Earth of the divine oneness of the Soul with God, and that happiness and contentment in this relation can only come when we have found for a mate one who believes as we believe and understands as we understand the deep significance and the sacred relation which was intended to be expressed in the marriage state. Hence we find the first miracle of Jesus performed at a marriage feast transmuting the waters of physical love into the wine of the spiritual union. With the help of our true mate we can literally not only recreate ourselves and bring into manifestation children who are so advanced as to be helpers in the world to spread this great truth, but we could also help to recreate the whole thought of mankind and ultimately bring about a greater manifestation of Divine Love on Earth instead of the inharmony and discord which now prevails.

After we have learned this, and after patiently waiting until we know we have found the one with whom we can bring about all this, we must have a better understanding of the sex relation. If we do not find our true mate we will know that it is because of our own failure to follow our inner guidance, either in this life or in the past. As long as we are calling evil that which has been foreordained to be the great lesson of this globe; as long as we refuse to bring the highest good out of it, we are turning our backs upon our Creator.

Remember that man has passed through many different experiences on different globes and on each globe there has been one particular lesson to learn. If there were nothing to learn out of the sex question then there would be no occasion for this globe to be created as it has been, ruled by the Law of Duality, and with the many ramifications of the sex problem in every department of Nature. Not a thing we see in Nature, with certain rare exceptions among microscopic forms of life, has come into life save through this dual manner of procreation. Therefore it is plain to those who think deeply that this is the main lesson for man to learn on this globe.

Nothing is evil of itself. That which seems to be evil is but a perversion of something which is Divine; for God never created evil. But man has in many cases covered up the Divine Spark with his own evil imaginings, and if he can find this Divinity and can purify this thing he calls evil and let it manifest only through love, then he will soon learn his lesson. Instead of struggling and antagonizing all the world because we are trying to do something that is unnatural and against God's law, we should say: "Here I find myself in a world that is not perfect. I find myself passing through a certain imperfect stage of unfoldment, so I must find out what the lesson is." The instant we say, "This thing is evil and I must kill it out or suppress it," then, because Nature has foreordained it, we either pervert or confine it to its lowest aspect; it manifests as lust, low desire, inharmony and a thousand other things, and thus retards all evolution. Even some advanced teachers advocate or condone practices which pervert that which in itself is the natural and normal expression of this force. In fact it becomes the opposite of God (Good) which is the devil or "d-evil" instead of Divine Love.

We cannot learn this great lesson without joining ourselves to Love, which is God. And by so doing we will have taken a step so much higher in evolution that the next lesson will be on a much higher plane.

We would advise you to study very carefully what is said on this subject in volume one of these Letters, in *The Key to the Universe* and in *The Voice of Isis*.

> "I have read a little on regeneration from *The Voice of Isis* and *Letters from the Teacher*, and understand that until the sex forces are transmuted I can make but little progress. Would you give me some instruction as to how to set about the transmutation of this force?"
> June 11, 1923.

The way to transmute the sex forces, or rather the way to begin this transmutation—for as you can gather from our literature this cannot be accomplished all at once, altho it is the ultimate completion of that which the human mechanism is intended to accomplish—is in lifting up all sexual thoughts into Divine Love. Transmutation does not mean suppression or refusal to use the usual normal functions which have been given to man, not because of a mistake, but because of the divine fiat which says, as was said in the beginning, "Be ye fruitful and multiply." But it does mean that all thought in connection with this question must be metaphorically laid upon the altar of the Most High and blessed.

Remember that we create and bring forth as much with our minds and our higher faculties as we do in any other way. So there is a very vital meaning in the words of Isaiah, "For more are the children of the desolate than the children of the married wife, saith the Lord," *i.e.*, we have more mental creations than physical.

Everyone who is striving to lift his thoughts up to the higher principles of Divine Love and understanding is in truth bringing forth children, which in times to come shall find expression upon the Earth and live as eternal principles, gradually perfecting more and more the inhabitants of the Earth. But we do not have to condemn our creative powers; those were given to us as a temporary means of peopling the Earth, both mentally, as we have tried to explain, as well as physically. And the only way to uplift and transmute these forces is to realize that there is a divine force back of it all; that we do create, whether it be by thoughts or by actual sexual manifestations, according to this Divine Principle back of it; or let us say, the Soul of it. There must be an uplifting desire to bring forth certain things that you know either are needed within yourself or in the world, such as love, purity, brotherhood, wisdom and a close touch with the Father, etc.

Therefore when you once get this understanding of

what is meant by creative power, you will see that it is not evil. But whether this sex desire expresses itself only within yourself as thoughts or whether it expresses itself between two perfectly mated people, man and wife, if the thought of evil comes into it, or the thought of self-indulgence, it creates evil instead of good. For remember this well, it creates after the inner mental vision if not after the flesh. Of course there are thousands of people who have been born after the flesh, but each one of us who is reaching the point where he is searching for Divinity has the great privilege of bringing forth after God's higher plan.

Of course you will understand perfectly that we cannot give physical bodies to Souls who desire to incarnate without using the function of sex intercourse, which God himself has given to His unfinished humanity to use and uplift and to bless. Yet very often an equal blessing adheres to those who, being unmarried, and consequently unable legally to bring forth physical bodies, nevertheless can, through their creative heart-love for the highest and the best, bring forth into actual manifestation in the world the love-children, let us call them, or the thoughts and principles which shall enter into the bodies that other people create. This is so badly needed owing to the ignorance with which most children are born and the curse which is thus put upon them by the wrong thought of their parents, and the dogma of the church that all children are born in sin, that if it were not so arranged that those desiring the highest and the best had this great privilege of uplifting many of these unfortunate children the prospect for humanity would be wellnigh hopeless and make it difficult for us to believe in the great love and justice of our Father-in-heaven. You are not asking anything that is harmful for you. Indeed, dear child, the very fact that your heart cries out and wants to know how to uplift this principle gives you the right to know. And we hope we have made it very plain that as long as you are an unmarried woman you must recognize the great blessing and the wonderful power of bringing forth ideal love, etc., which can be broadcasted and showered upon the children who are without it. Later on, when you have a husband who is your own true mate, you can put these same love thoughts and desires and holy principles into the act of sex intercourse and thus bring forth children who are blessed from their birth and from whom the curse of the man-made idea of the evil of sexual intercourse is removed.

The whole question is one of the most vital that man can consider and the principal one that is to be faced and answered by the inhabitants of this globe. Therefore you can see you are not to be blamed for wanting to know. Moreover, God is a God of Love and He never punishes His children or His loved ones because they are ignorantly following only the law of the flesh, even though they must reap the ensuing Karma. But He longs to have them follow the law of the Spirit, the inner Divine Law. St. Paul says: "I delight in the law of God after the inward man." But he also says: "When I would do good, evil is present with me."[1] Altho we can never excuse ourselves for letting the evil dominate, nevertheless we know that God will not condemn us for the slips and mistakes we have made.

---

[1] *Romans*, VII, 21-2.

> "I thank you for the explanation of my dream. I was rather surprised, yet it gave me the key to much that I am striving for at the present time. We have tried hard to follow the ideal of Spiritual Companions in our marriage, but without much success or happiness."
>
> Oct. 18, 1922.

As to you and your husband striving to fulfill the marriage relation in purity, etc., we wonder if you fully understand what is meant by purity. We ask that you read very carefully the chapter on Purity and also the Appendix in *The Voice of Isis*, which treats of this subject quite fully.

There is no more fruitful source of inharmony and disruption to family ties than the idea that all sexual intercourse is impure and to be killed out and destroyed. *God never made anything to be killed out.* To purify a thing means to see it in its highest light and use it for its highest purpose, in this case to come together in perfect love and purity of thought.

As we said, God never made anything to be killed out. The truth is that this problem of sexual intercourse is the mighty problem which the inhabitants of this planet are intended to solve. And only when it is fully solved—not trampled out and killed, for it never can be killed, but should be truly purified and uplifted and made the foundation for all higher understanding—will their eyes be able to see that which is beyond. We feel that ere you can pluck the lilies in the beautiful ponds of your vision, which you pass in your physical journey, you must not only leave behind several pairs of old shoes (old shoes are that which once covered your understanding but have now worn out), but literally renew your understanding and purify your ideas. For as long as we call anything which God has created unclean or wicked we are making ourselves judges of that which we know, little about. "What God has cleansed that call not thou unclean."

> "My husband and I have both long ago decided to live a life of celibacy; it was hard at first, but now we seem to be growing into it. We thank you for all your help to make us understand."
> Jan. 16, 1923.

As to your remark in regard to celibacy, if you feel the need by all means follow it. You know you will always have our help and advice and that we do not try either to coerce or to force our pupils to follow our ideas. We not only give them the privilege but urge them to follow out to its utmost any thought which comes to them as the best and wisest; then after trying it, if they need further advice, we are glad to help them.

However, we must admit that we do not think that God Almighty made such a terrible mistake when He created man and woman as separate sexes and gave as His command "Be ye fruitful and multiply." Yet we know there are many teachers who believe they could have made this world very much better and could have multiplied and replenished the Earth and have brought forth in a much more attractive way. And those who think so should at least have a chance to prove it. Whichever decision, however, they come to, we know they must not leave God out of it nor try to defy His laws nor call them impure; for what God hath made, He Himself in the presence of the angelic hosts, declared "Behold, all is good."

We are truly glad that you feel that the Order has helped you at least a step onward toward complete purification. We will continue to send you this purifying force and to sympathize with and try to understand your needs in the phase of development in which you are at present. Complete purification means first to purify the body, then to purify the mind; then when the body and mind are both pure, to let the purification sink down into the heart, into the secret chamber where God stands; to look into the great marvelous Eye of Wisdom and without shrinking say, "Lo, I am pure." But, dear children, each one must follow his own guidance. Some must walk one way; some must walk another way; for there is one universal law given to all alike, which is "Judge not." For no man knows why or under what conditions a person needs the lesson through which he is passing. No doubt you are doing your best, but try to believe that all others who are walking in the path are also trying to do their best. As to helping you further, there are certain mental veils which must be lifted before we can help you further. But we are always close to you and ready to catch your hand if you should slip; to explain, if you no longer understand; to answer, when you have been able to formulate the problem which alone will bring you understanding.

> "With reference to your advice as to the necessity of fulfilling the marriage relation in love and perfect parity, we only now truly understand what you mean. I presume this is one of the mental veils which we had to lift. We know you will be glad, as well as we, that the Great White Light has at last broken through."
> May 3, 1923.

We are very glad you are seriously taking up this most important question of sex. Our Teachings are so different from the average teachings that it is difficult to combat the idea which so many have, *i.e.*, that sex is but something to be killed out. However, we are sure that now you are started on the subject you will see the reasonableness and the vital necessity of recognizing the fact that nothing is conquered that has not been turned to its highest use.

There should be no such thing as killing out or destroying anything that God has made. And in this present life we must give an account of every faculty and function with which we find ourselves endowed; we must come back to it again and again until we can really say "It is finished." Nor is it ever finished until the snake which now crawls upon the ground and which has become all white, has become uplifted into the Rod of Power by which we can manifest our sonship with the divine Christ.

All your dreams had to do with this subject and they all show that you are trying to deal with it. Keep on trying, for it is a very vital question. The fact that the . . . . have not solved it is proved by the fact that it has not brought happiness, harmony or peace or helpfulness, either to the Society or to individual members. Whenever it is necessary for man to invent a substitute for that which God has intended to be, as we have said, lifted up into the Rod of Power, then we should know we are on the wrong track; for whatever man makes as a substitute becomes vile and impure.

> "Thank you for the exact interpretation of my dream. We have just seen that prophecy, *i.e.*, that our source of esoteric instruction had been poisoned by the snake. My husband has had a dream which plainly showed him that the current in which he was swimming was so polluted that it was wise for him to climb out. We found the answer as we studied your Letters from the Teacher on the sex problem."
> March 24, 1923.

When you say that the former source of your esoteric wisdom had been poisoned, you must remember that altho in a measure this was true, yet the real source of esoteric wisdom is reached through your true and earnest desire to receive from the Divine.

Therefore, if one channel proves unworthy, you are always brought into contact with another. This never fails, for no Soul who has decided to take up the truly earnest study of esoteric wisdom is ever left without a helper; not only a helper in the higher realms, but he will be led to the source from which he will get the esoteric wisdom without poison, clean and true and sincere.

We are very glad that the dream about your husband was true. Of course it is needless for us to repeat that our Teachings do not in any way corroborate the idea that celibacy is at all necessary, but *purification* is, and a realization that all love is Divine, is the only source from which that which we call sex can ever bring forth in perfect purity and love. Of course there will come a time when all of us who have learned this great lesson of life will perhaps reincarnate on some other planet where celibacy is the desirable state. But at present we are here, and the purification of sex through true love is the great lesson to learn. And we will never reach a higher standard — any more than we will reach a higher standard on the use of money, etc. — until we learn that God in His wisdom and love has given us these lessons in a world which is built up to solve just these problems.

Therefore the best way to reach what we feel to be the desired end is to fulfill to our utmost all the lessons that confront us here and now, knowing well that we are not expected, while passing through this phase of our development, to reach and understand others, any more than a child graduating from the grammar school is expected to be able to answer questions or to express the knowledge he will later learn when he goes to college.

> "Will you please give me a clearer understanding of what is meant in your lesson "The Initiation of Job as to the twain being one soul? Also about Behemoth eating grass like an ox."
>
> May 3, 1922.

As to the quotation from our lesson, "Up to this time the twain who are one have shared the same experiences," etc., we were speaking of the time previous to the middle of the Third Race, at which time the sexes separated. Up to that time the two sexes were in one body, but that was *not yet a physical body*, but an ethereal or semi-physical body. During that semiphysical life, being one they naturally had the same experiences. And altho after the sexes separated each had to have his or her own experience, nevertheless the vague Soul-memory of that time when both belonged together will always remain and help attract the one to the other. But each has to perfect his or her own spiritual unfoldment through experiences in the physical for which each may have to go a different path for a time. But some day, since they have really started out as one Soul, they must again join together in a higher life when the physical has been transcended. But there will never be two Souls in one *physical* body, as that dual manifestation was but an ethereal expression when the bodies were not physical, but ethereal. Therefore they will never manifest in one body until they are once more super-physical and ethereal.

The quotation you give about Behemoth eating grass, etc., is a symbolic expression. As we have said, Behemoth and Leviathan are simply mystical presentations of the great force of attraction between the sexes, in this present life often degraded as it manifests upon the physical plane. Behemoth eating grass as an ox symbolizes that as long as the force is used merely as an animal function it will be fed by the lower conditions instead of by the higher and spiritual. This means that the sex function must not be considered simply as a physical animal function, altho it points out that through man's mistakes he has degraded this greatest of all spiritual forces until it is largely looked upon as merely an animal attraction between the sexes. This is intended as a warning that as we thus degrade this mighty force we deliberately create in ourselves bestiality.

> "A beautiful young woman, being in love with love, was swept off her feet by the magnetism of a powerful and handsome man and married him. After the first night she discovered her mistake. Of a highly refined, pure and modest nature his physical demands upon her shocked her into almost hatred. Her whole nature revolted. She knows something of your Teachings, but wishes to know more on this subject. She longs for pure love and happiness, but feels that her Soul is being desecrated daily. Must she continue to submit to that which so revolts her?"

Tell your friend to listen to the Inner Voice which is speaking to her so plainly, for it speaks Divine Truth. We would advise her to have a plain talk with her husband and tell him that henceforth she was to be the master of her own body, for women are no longer the chattels of their husbands. Tell her that his marriage vow was "to love and CHERISH her and if he does not do that, if he keeps her chiefly to minister to his lust, he has already broken his vow and therefore cannot hold her to it if she wishes to ask the law to complete her freedom. The Divine Law is that "Whom God hath joined, no man can put asunder," but that God knows who belong together and tells us in one way or another if we will but listen and obey.

If we have made a mistake then we have not been joined by God, only by an outer man-made ceremony which man can also annul. And certainly God never intended her merely to be a convenient fulfillment of any man's lust. Tell her that when it is only the outer human personalities that are joined and the true marriage is not made in heaven or in a true spiritual union, such a union is but legalized prostitution, as nothing can sanction sexual intercourse save true love and harmony. A union of lust and degradation is monstrous, almost enough to sully her Soul. And since God could not sanction such a union, no matter what outer ceremony was performed, all the laws of purity and good cry out against it.

Tell her also that only the pure, true love she has kept alive in her heart has saved her from the pit of degradation which her husband has digged for her feet. Tell her to place the problem on the altar of the Most High and then follow her guidance after sincere prayer for such direction. Then let her calmly trust God to lead her in due season to that which is her own. If she is thus trustful and resigned her own will come to her in some life if not in this, altho even the latter is possible if she keeps herself pure for his sake. Tell her that every embrace of lust but creates barriers which will put off the fulfillment of God's divine plan for her and for her own.

> "I made the acquaintance of a young man and fell deeply in love with him and he with me. After our friendship was well on the way I found he was married; but my love was so deep that I feel he belongs more to me than to her, as they are misfits. I feel sorry for her. I know I cannot hope to belong to him on the earth plane, but is it wrong to meet him as a friend, for I feel sure we are Soul-mates."
> Nov. 3, 1923.

If you will read what is said on die subject in *The Key to the Universe*, under number 3, you will see that we have stated that it matters not how close you are or how sure you are that a person is your Soul-mate, if he belongs to another and you cannot have him in this life it means that a certain Karma has separated you. And if you try to deceive yourself by thinking it is right to have a certain intimacy on the physical plane, as long as you do not permit it to go to greater lengths, you run the risk of putting off the union with your mate in the next incarnation. If, as you believe, you are true mates you can well afford to wait until the barriers are removed.

We are sorry to have to tell you this, but it would not help you to let you deceive yourself in this matter. Therefore, you must consider very carefully whether or not you are real mates. If so he is yours for all eternity, whether temporarily separated or not. If you make this decision and adhere to it you know not how quickly the freedom may come, even in this life.

If, as you say, he and his wife are misfits, then she is probably as unhappy with him as he is with her and she would probably be quite ready for a divorce. For again, it is practically impossible for the Souls who are not mated to live together as man and wife and be happy. However, as long as they do live together they must be true to each other, for nothing can excuse the violation of the marriage vow. Therefore talk to him and ask him if he loves you enough to propose a legal separation from his wife. If he refuses, then put him out of your mind, for he is not worthy of your love. But if he is willing to do so, then it should be put up to her, and if she consents and if the law, which is always a third party in the marriage contract, also consents, then he can be free to become not only spiritually but legally married on Earth to the one who is really his.

All this is perhaps not what you would call comforting, but it is Truth, and no amount of so-called comfort or advice can be given by the Masters to any human being except that which is eternally true and that which they know will bring a solution of the difficulty in the best possible way. Remember, no condition ever exists that has not been created by the persons themselves. Also, it is quite possible that if you determinedly separate yourself from his influence for a time you may find he is not your Soul-mate at all, but simply a karmic companion, and then you will be glad you waited and found out before complicating matters further.

> "I have a great problem to lay before you. My boy, 19, tells me he is in love with a girl of not very good character. She is now pregnant and it is laid upon my boy. Will the Teacher tell me if it is a desirable thing that he should marry her, as he earnestly wants to."
>
> Aug. 22, 1923.

Your problem is not only a personal one, but is also a world problem, and for this reason it is most important that it be decided according to the divine way of looking at things rather than merely making it a question of your own happiness or of any personal prejudice against it.

There is no question but that your boy has broken the Law of Divine Love and Harmony and must some time, either in this life or in some other, pay the karmic debt. At this particular time in the world's history humanity fails to realize the great importance the overcoming of mere sex attraction. The only way and the karmic necessity for truth in love matters and any of us will learn this great lesson is by determinedly doing what seems to be the right thing and trusting in the Divine Lord of Life to bring to us that which is best.

We know your boy is very young. We know he has been associated with a class of people who would laugh at any so-called sentimental ideals in connection with this matter. We also realize that his desire to marry the girl is a beautiful indication of his higher ideals pushing to the front and seeking to overcome the flesh; nevertheless we see plainly that from an earthly standpoint this might be looked upon simply as foolish weakness. Yet were he to feel this to be foolish weakness and treat this girl with scorn he would be adding his mite to the terrible karmic burden under which the entire world today is struggling.

The sex problem is one great avenue through which the light of Divine Love must permeate the darkness of earthly misconception and ultimately bring to the understanding of humanity the realization that Love is not passion; that it is in reality divine redemption. And when we say divine redemption we mean it in its deepest sense. Even those who sin in this respect and who determinedly seek to overcome and suffer in the overcoming are learning this greatest of all lessons, namely, THE LESSON for which this globe was created; the lesson the inhabitants of this globe must learn and overcome before they are ready to go on to a higher and happier development upon some other globe. This is, we might say, the Law back of the whole question.

Now, let us look at the thing from a more personal point of view. It is just possible that he really loves this girl, and if so all things can be forgiven if he marries her. Again, it is just possible that she loves him and that because of his trust in her and his desire to help her to do right she may be redeemed from whatever evil has taken place in the past; and they may be very happy together. This often occurs, for, as we said before, love is the great redeemer of the world; and while it sometimes redeems through suffering it ultimately brings understanding and peace. Yet it also redeems through the striving to do the right thing because, in spite of all, there is Love. If so, no social prejudices should stand in the way of marriage.

Our advice would be to see both the boy and the girl and talk to them after this fashion. Strive to find out first if they do love each other and are ready to join their lives in one of love, or if the marriage would be but one of compulsion. If it is only that, we believe it would be better not to permit it, but to let them suffer; yet we do not think it right to let the girl suffer alone, as both are equally guilty in the sight of God. But we do think you should have a plain talk and an understanding with both. There should also be an understanding of your husband's attitude, and in talking the matter over with him put it before him in the same sense of a world's problem. He should face the thing bravely, for just as in the *Bible* story where they were stoning the young woman for a like crime and Jesus said, "He that is without sin among you, let him first cast a stone at her," so you should say to him, and if he can answer, "I am without sin," then say to him, "With all my heart I permit you to cast the first stone at my boy and yours."

> "I have read that the Soul of man is feminine and the Soul of woman masculine. Is this so? I always had the impression that the Soul was sexless."

As a matter of fact sex inheres in the Soul itself, or let us rather say that the Soul embraces both sexes in potentiality, but in the world of duality (earth) must express them separately. Thus when a man sees a vision of his Higher Self it always appears in a feminine form because he himself is manifesting the masculine aspect. He is therefore more easily touched and awakened through a vision which is feminine, and it would always seem to him more helpful than would a masculine form. For the same reason when a woman sees a vision of her Higher Self it appears to be masculine. Yet, as we said, the Soul is dual-sexed, hence can appear as either masculine or feminine.

As to the Soul on the astral plane, it is just what it is on the physical plane. Therefore on the astral plane it would have just the same appearance as on the physical plane. The Soul is always Divine and its home is on the *spiritual*, not the astral, plane. When such a vision comes it comes to bring to you a recognition of the higher spiritual part of you, not the astral part. While on the physical plane we are more apt to hear its voice interiorly as the still, small voice, or perhaps feel its great urge toward higher and more spiritual actions; and sometimes in answer to our longings for something better or in answer to our prayers.

> "I have been taught by . . . . that no ego has more than seven lives to live in one sex nor fewer than three. Now, judging from what I have read in your *Voice of Isis* this appears to be fallacious. I am a woman, but feel positively that I was a man in my past life."
>
> March 31, 1923.

The Soul itself, being dual sexed, under the Law of Duality, naturally inclines to express each sex in a separate physical habiliment or physical body. And it would always do this were it to go on without making any Karma which necessitated a change. Unfortunately tho there are many reasons which make it necessary for the Soul to change; for instance, if it was a masculine aspect of the Soul which had despised woman and tried to rise superior to her, it often must incarnate as a woman to learn the lesson that both sexes are equal but opposite. But only when some such special reason for the change exists does the Soul change the sex of its body. Yet it is always easy to understand the real sex of the Soul if you carefully watch the person. We all know the masculine type of woman who in reality should be a man; we also know the feminine type of man who should be a woman, yet has incarnated as a man.

You see, we differ greatly in this teaching from the Society, and we think our teaching is corroborated by Nature. No doubt the fact that you were so determined not to be a woman is because you were a man in the past life, and perhaps in that incarnation you learned the lesson which had caused you to make the mistake. Either that or it was in the last life that you made the mistake—of despising women—which compelled you to be born a woman in this life. If it is the former, then you can redeem the past by learning the great lesson of the equality of the sexes and by cultivating your true womanly nature. If, however, it is the latter condition, namely, that you are a woman today because you despised women in the past, then you must learn that lesson in every way you can think of, which will teach you what a true woman should be, and all her great responsibilities of leading the world into spiritual paths, etc.

As long as you keep on saying you are too strong and positive a nature to be happy as a woman, you will continue to be a woman. But when you say: "I will set to work with all my might, with the help of the Living Christ, to learn my lessons and to overcome, or rather, direct and train my positive nature," or let us say what is more true, "Let the Divine Light of true love soften my nature." Then you can be very sure that the greater the effort you put forth through love, the sooner will you go back to your own sex, and you will then manifest it with that softening quality that this change of sex was intended to bring you. Remember, however, that we do not mean love for any special personality, but letting the Divine Love fill you and teach you.

Moreover, another thing is apt to bring about change of sex and it is very apt to come to one who is of that positive and strong nature that you seem to be. It is the idea of the superiority of the masculine sex over the feminine. And at this particular time when the suffragettes and women agitators are so rampant, many who are taking this destructive view of the subject have at one time been men and have brought about just the conditions which women today are rising in their might to correct. Nor could anyone else accomplish it. One who had always been a woman would not feel that strong aggressive masculine opposition to what they had found to be oppression and unjust treatment.

So take all these ideas into consideration and ask sincerely what is the lesson for you; then set to work to learn it and so make sure this will be your last feminine incarnation.

> "Will you please tell me why man had to wait until the middle of the third race for the division of the sexes, while all other forms of life are bisexual? Are not men and women equally guilty in committing adultery?"
>
> July 18, 1923.

Evidently you do not understand just what is meant by the Races. The First and the Second and the beginning of the Third Race were not physical at all, but were astral or semi-physical, and in them neither man, insect nor animal existed in the dense physical form as we know them today. The Earth was in the process of formation, and man, a semi-astral being not yet physical, was not yet separated into sexes. The middle of the Third Race is the period at which the *Bible* history takes up man, "Male and female created He them." And Adam and Eve represented this great Third Race in which the separation of the sexes occurred.

As to whether men and women are not equally guilty in committing adultery, they are equal. Yet in some cases the woman is the more guilty for the very reason that woman has the intuitions of the Divine Mother-force and this should bring an inner sense of purity and higher appreciation of what is meant by the joining of the sexes. Moreover because of the overshadowing of the Divine Mother-force woman should have a far truer insight into the meaning of true love and the necessity of passing through this sex expression for the purpose of lifting up and purifying the earthly atoms and making them capable of really bringing forth Divinity in the earthly particles of the globe and in humanity. Therefore, according to the Law of Life that the one most capable of understanding is the one most responsible, we would be apt to say that the female would be the most to blame.

However, according to the Law of the Higher Life, condemnation has no place. We must judge all people by the amount of unfoldment and the power of understanding that they possess. Woman, being overshadowed by the great force of the Divine Mother, the Bringer-forth of the universe, has within her greater possibilities of spiritual understanding. Yet if she will not look within, or because of wrong religious teaching and condemnation of the whole question as a wrong idea, then she is no more culpable than the man, for in such a case she knows no better, especially if the man knows more about the use of such forces than she does. Always the one most blameable is the one who knows the most of the real use and ultimate benefit this force should bring to the world.

> "What I want to know most of all is, is it right for a woman, a student of any occult school, to be obliged to force her body into the marriage relation? If the marriage is fulfilling the Law of Compensation is it right to drive your body to fill the needs of another?"
> March 20, 1923.

Although we know there are many occult schools, in fact the majority, that teach the doctrine of celibacy, we do not believe in it or teach it. We base our understanding of this fact upon the Law as expressed in Nature and in all truly spiritual teachings. We feel that if the marriage relation did not contain a necessary lesson for humanity while passing through this particular phase of unfoldment, then a God of Love and wisdom would never have made such a temptation, or let us say, such a function, as an avenue of expression of the laws which are manifesting through the entire planet. For we find that this sex manifestation is given not only to man but to all created things on the planet as a fundamental law. And only as we absolutely do not deny, but fulfill the law, can we reach Mastery, or let us say, become one with the Law.

No one who demands such a thing as the denying of this function can possibly fulfill the Law, therefore we must use commonsense to find out how to fulfill the Law. And when we do this we find we must fulfill the Law in love. Therefore, love, which is God and which we are told is the fulfilling of the Law, is the purifying influence which makes this thing not only possible but commendable. He who loves most draws closest to God and if we try to have marriage without the marriage relation we are shutting the door on one of man's highest expressions of love; hence are shutting God outside.

Therefore, we believe that the lesson given to humanity to learn from this act is one of love, obedience and a realization that there is nothing impure, nothing that, if performed rightly, can harm either the body or the mind or the spiritual advance of any student who is drawing close to God in His aspect of Divine Love.

We cannot study this universe without grasping the thought that for some great and marvelous reason this particular planet has been created for the manifestation of the two opposite sexes. We see it in all things, but exemplified most strongly in man. It becomes unclean only when man himself lends to it his lower unclean thoughts and forgets that he, being the Lord of creation, is expected to uplift this great thought and make it really a drawing close to God in Divine Love. God Himself in His manifold creations has cleansed it and therefore those of us who want to be God's children and do His will perfectly dare not call it unclean; if there is anything which God has cleansed and we call it unclean, then we are bound to that thing.

Some day when man has learned this great lesson, doubtless we shall inhabit a globe on which procreation takes place in some other manner. But we are not expected to live in the future and we dare not leave any lesson unlearned now. We shall conquer it only when we have cleansed it through Divine Love and manifest it in love. These are our Teachings and we feel that all the realms of Nature uphold us in them.

Chapter XII

MARRIAGE AND DIVORCE

> "How shall I find the proper person to marry?"
> Sept 7, 1922.

If you listen to the inner guidance and pray earnestly to know whether any certain person to whom you are greatly attracted is the right one, the guidance will be given you in one way or another. It is only those who do not ask for or who refuse to follow their Divine Guidance who make mistakes in marriages.

In all our years of experience with problems of this kind we have yet to find a mismated couple who did not acknowledge that some time during the courtship they had had a strong inner warning against the marriage. Often such a warning is not heeded lest the breaking of the engagement cause a social jar and temporary mental anguish. Yet such temporary suffering as may occur is as nothing as compared to the years of suffering to which they condemn themselves in a loveless or mistaken marriage.

If you have no one in mind then wait patiently for that which the Great Law has in store for you. Far better wait than create the Karma of a mistaken marriage.

> "I have met a young lady who to me seems to be surely my true mate, but we have each had our horoscopes made and from their reading we are told that astrologically we should not marry. Can you help us, as we both love deeply?"
> July 4, 1923.

In the case of Soul-mates we take no special account of the astrological indications. Each Soul has his own true Soul-mate, *i.e.*, some time in the very beginning of their evolution the two were one, and although they are not necessarily married to each other in every incarnation (because sometimes one has some lesson which must be learned alone), or the other is not in incarnation; nevertheless they must ultimately come together again and must work out their complete Karma together. They would always be together if they always followed their higher guidance and sought always for help from on high.

Every Soul that comes to this world must pass through all the signs of the zodiac at least twelve times. Therefore you can understand that two Souls destined to be one might at some point in their evolution be manifesting through different zodiacal signs. But if they had obeyed the Law and had always worked together they might be in exactly the right signs.

Regardless of the astrological aspects, if you have asked for guidance the guidance will be given you, and if you are reasonably sure that you are mates then the marriage is right. If your signs are not favorable it simply means that you will both have karmic stumbling-blocks to overcome. But these last only for this life, and the great love between you will help you to overcome them. In looking forward to your marriage, instead of asking whether or not you are mated astrologically, ask that you be shown beyond any mistake whether or not you truly belong together and are complementary Souls.

"A man is married by law to one who is not his true spiritual mate. Under these circumstances is not that man free to give other expression, entirely apart from any physical contact at all, of a true spiritual love? After a

> divorce might not the two mates live together, always provided it was entirely apart from any physical expression?"
>
> Oct. 28, 1922.

We would say that if two persons are married and yet are not absolutely mated, they have a certain Karma to fulfill and they must fulfill it as man and wife in all that this implies. However, when this Karma is once fulfilled, then they should have a plain understanding and agree to secure their freedom. But remember that there are three parties to the contract, namely, the man, the woman and the law of the land (not having been joined together by the Divine Law), and all three of these must release the bond.

If either after or before this release the man should meet his true mate, he is not free to marry that one until the release is consummated. As to living together without any physical connection we believe this is almost impossible and beyond the power given to man to accomplish. It is by no means a sin to have this conjugal relation; but there is much misunderstanding of this law of Good. The celibate life is but a farce, and there is really no such thing upon this plane. Those who pretend to it or strive for it and are not truly celibate in their thoughts are adding to their Karma a falsity which must ultimately be redeemed in some life, and with bitter suffering.

To surround children with the thought that all children are "born in sin" is to make it so. To say that all sexual relation is vile and to be overcome is to make it vile. But if it is looked upon as something which expresses the highest that man in his present stage of development can reach or grasp of the real Divine Creative Life-force, then it becomes the greatest opportunity for man, not only to attract to this Earth Divine Souls, but also to create Godlike pos-

abilities and powers in the lives and bodies of each. However, should those who desire this advance not be married, they must realize that for some reason their Karma has not fitted them to do this great work. And they must do the best they can to purify their celibate lives and to wait until the Karma which they have made in the past on this subject, is completely worked out. This can only be when they have learned to think correctly on the subject and realize that this life is given to them to prepare them in purity of thought and higher aspiration and perfect understanding to take up the work thus outlined.

Nothing that has been given to mankind has been given as a punishment or as a temptation for him to sink deeper in sin. But this great test which has been given to the people of this Earth, alone of all the planets, is the greatest test ever before given to man, and man has degraded it. We know well that to kill out anything God has made and given to us is a sin; it becomes a terrible "Dweller on the Threshold" for humanity to overcome. And only by the few who can see more deeply and look within the very heart of the subject and reason it out and determine to work it out, can even the beginning of this purification be undertaken. And yet it is the task which some day must be learned either in this humanity or in one to come.

> "Have you any lessons upon the attainment of two Souls to the same vibration, one positive and the other negative? This I understand is analogous to unity with God. Can these two Souls attain Mastery without working together in the flesh?"
> Jan. 31, 1923.

If by chance two people marry who are both posited to the same vibration, they are affinities and not mates, for they are just alike; both are strong in the same way and both are weak at the same points. But if they are posited to the opposite poles, then each is a complement of the other and they are most helpful and necessary to each other. One will then be strong where the other is weak and weak where the other is strong.

Those who get married and afterwards find they must separate, altho at first they seemed to be in love, are those who are posited to the same vibration or who were drawn together by propinquity, by physical desire or karmic ties. Such soon find out they do not really belong together and the happiness of married life soon ceases.

Soul-mates cannot attain complete mastery unless working together. But very often one has advanced beyond the other, hence must wait, perhaps out of incarnation, until the other one has faced and overcome whatever they have left undone or that holds them back. Then in the next life they will be together; for ultimately they must conquer as one.

> "Will you please explain to me why you make a difference between what you call Soul-mates and affinities?"
>
> Sept. 16, 1922.

Affinities are two beings who are alike, while Soul-mates are opposites; that is, in Soul-mates one is strong where the other is weak, and weak where the other is strong. Consequently they fulfill each other just as two halves of an apple make one complete whole. Affinities, however, would be like half a sweet apple and half a sour apple which could never be united to make one perfect whole.

Also affinities seldom succeed in remaining together, or, if they do, can never bring happiness, any more than the sides of two separate mussel shells can ever be united to make a dwelling-place for a living creature. Affinities may make excellent friends but never satisfactory mates.

> "I have a very strong impression which seems to be corroborated by my horoscope and many other things, that in my past incarnation I was of the opposite sex. Will you please tell me if this is truer."
>
> Feb. 28, 1923.

We have found that it is no kindness to tell a pupil about past incarnations, hence we are not permitted to do so. However, if the scenes and circumstances of the past are brought to you, corroborated by the horoscope, historical events, etc., it is evidently for a purpose. Therefore ask of the Divine for guidance in the use of this material, that the best good may come therefrom.

It is quite possible that you are a masculine Soul temporarily incarnated in a feminine body. If so, there will be many things to corroborate it besides your early indignation at being a girl. This would also explain many of the conditions you have had to meet and which have been so puzzling to you. Do not, however, let your mind dwell constantly on this thought, for by doing so you may so mix up your Karma that you will not get the full benefit of the lessons of this present life. Therefore, ask for guidance; pray earnestly that whatever is true shall work out in your life. Then live your life as tho you had no such inner suspicion of the change of sex, else in the next life the discrepancy may be even more pronounced.

> "About four years ago I met a man in a most strange and remarkable way. He had been a . . . .for twenty years. We all had con-

sidered him a Master, a Saint, so highly developed did he appear; and his complete indifference to all that makes up life and its suffering made us think he had overcome all human weakness . . . . but he did many things that the world would call unfair . . . . He lived in my house and we studied together for a long time. Our friends insisted on calling us 'twin souls which are blessed to have met', yet since his first letters after going to America he has refused to answer my letters for nearly a year. Has Karma decided our final separation?"

As to your dilemma in regard to the man who claims to be a Master, in one sense it is a natural one. In fact, so common are such experiences that if not so serious they would provoke a smile. It is so easy for persons to get the reputation of Mastery among Souls who are eagerly looking for something better and higher and who are over-ready to give adulation to those who claim it.

There are certain laws which proclaim a Master. The first and foremost of these is absolute humility and refusal to permit adulation. A Master would rebuke most positively all attempts of the rest of humanity to put Him upon a pedestal; He would know so thoroughly the weakness of the human heart and that such adulation and false acclaim would tend to pull Him down from His high estate, provided such had been attained and that it would hold back His followers from attaining Mastery themselves. A real Master would be above such adoration.

"Perfect indifference to the sufferings of others" does not by any means proclaim Mastery. True Mastery knows so thoroughly the weakness and the intense suffering of the little ones who have not yet conquered, that the Masters have all compassion, all tender consideration. This consideration may not be given in words or in condemnation or in so-called instruction, but it is felt. Their very presence brings relief and peace and calm. Enough said on this point. Such a person is by no means a Master.

If this man were your twin soul and necessary to your life here upon the physical plane he would be with you. He would not have been taken from you to save you from further wreck of your ideals and your understandings and your principles. Lay him upon the altar of the Law. And when we say this we mean that you should recognize that there is a Divine Law-giver, a mighty living Principle which we call God, who rules the universe and rules the hearts of all the atoms in the universe; that each atom is brought into contact with the conditions best suited for its growth and development. Therefore, if it were right for you to have the man you speak of with you he would be there. The truth is that he has been deliberately taken away and kept away that you may learn other lessons and understand greater principles. Believe absolutely that if the time should come when your spiritual perfection needed him, or if he were *really* your complementary mate and you were ready to go on together, you would be together.

So do not call him back, but ask simply that this great Divine Law shall guard both him and you and bring to each of you just the lessons, the forces and the powers of life which shall bring each of you to perfection. Then tell yourself that this mighty Principle of life and love needs the perfection of both your Souls and bodies, both yours and his, far more than you can possibly desire his love or his perfection. For without the perfection of either one of you the universe is to that extent manifesting incompletely, and all the forces of the universe are put forth to bring you to your ultimate destiny, which is this perfection. Believe this. Trust in it. Follow it. Make no effort to bring to yourself something which has been taken from you by the Great Law, knowing that if it is necessary for you to have it, it will be brought back; and if it is not necessary or is not God's will, then you do not want it. To want it or to demand it is to interfere with this Great Law. When you once realize this, you will rest in peace.

We ask you to repeat the *Prayer of Protection* and the *Prayer for Light*. And as you say this *Prayer for Light*, fill your whole mind with the thought of what this Light and living force is and try to manifest it, try to radiate it to all conditions and know that as long as you are willing to work with this Law and rest in this Light all things needed for your joy and happiness will be brought to you in due time.

> "There is a powerful attraction for me in Algiers, greatly intensified by the fact that I became deeply attracted to a young Arabian just before coming away. If he were a European I would not hesitate to marry him. As he is an Arab I do not know if it is wise to place myself under influences which might be difficult to cope with."
> March 9, 1923.

If two Souls belong to each other and have this yearning for union, it matters not whether one is Arabian and the other English or of any other nationality. Remember that all Souls have to pass through many experiences and many nationalities, and if they cannot pass through these experiences with sympathy or cannot correlate mentally with the different national characteristics, then they have to incarnate in countries quite foreign to their natures. This is one cause. Another is that there are Souls so balanced and yet so desirous of touching the inner Soul experiences and qualities of nations quite opposite to their own that they will deliberately incarnate in such nations.

We feel that this is the case with you and your Arabian friend. Therefore if after praying sincerely and earnestly for guidance you still feel that your love for him and his for you is sufficient to bridge the national and racial differences between you, have no fear; for he may be your mate, and if so, you will be happy with him no matter what the racial differences may be. This period of separation has doubtless been sent to you purposely to prove to you whether it is a mere infatuation due to personality and romance, or whether it is a really deep Soul tie. Consider it prayerfully and earnestly. And when you pray about it, go to the Christ as a Divine friend: ask that you may be shown and then wait for your answer. The answer will probably not come in words, but there will be some event or happening which will be so convincing that you will know at once whether he is or is not your mate. Do not make the mistake of thinking that if he is your mate, then at once all differences in opinion and racial characteristics will disappear. They will not. But your love will help you to bridge these differences and make you happy in spite of them.

> "We had only been married five months when we quarreled. He stamped and slammed and swore. He treated me as a child, as if I did not know anything. I fear I have made a great mistake. His ways and my ways are not at all alike. Can you help me?"

Sept. 19, 1923.

Dear child, it is too soon as yet to come to any drastic conclusion. Our advice is to go bravely to your husband and talk to him plainly and understandingly, and without giving way to impatience or temper and ask him what he thinks about it and how he feels. We do not feel that our writing to him would in any way better conditions and it might make them far worse. It was a mistake to go away and leave him without an explanation, for very often in the early days of married life just such quarrels and misunderstandings crop up. And they would ultimately be overcome by love if both of you had the courage to bear them for a little while and would carefully note your own faults and see where you were to blame, instead of blaming it all on the other; for it takes two to make a quarrel, and generally both are at fault.

Try to remember the love you felt for him before marriage which made you desire him for a husband. And when you go to him, go in the spirit that this love awoke in you at the time; with a willingness to admit your own mistakes. Ask him if he is ready to meet you half way or if love is indeed dead. There is nothing so terrible as a separation which comes simply from a misunderstanding or a lack of patient waiting. Remember there are very few people in this world who never lose their tempers.

Therefore, dear child, after you have prayed earnestly over the question and have asked the Lord Christ to enter into you and to purify you from all impatience and unworthiness and to give you the courage to speak the truth, then go and talk to your husband. After this test, and we would say after a little longer trial of married life, if you find some vital major obstacle that is impossible to ignore, it will be time enough to conclude that you have made a mistake in your marriage.

Married life requires much patience; much giving and forgiving; a great deal of praying and striving to make your own life what it should be. Often those who are in reality true mates find it most difficult to get along because they are opposites and look at problems from an opposite direction. And naturally unless both have been touched by the wand of Divine Love, each thinks his side of the question is the only right one. Only when we have learned that the two halves are always different, yet that it takes the two halves to make one whole, are we ready to know whether we have made a great mistake or whether the experience is only to teach us a lesson: which, if we refuse to accept and work out, will bring us greater sorrow and disaster than if we try with all our heart to learn the lesson which is intended for us.

Chapter XIII

DISCOURAGEMENT

> "I have a great longing to live only the religions life, yet my husband, my children, and so many petty duties hold me back. Can you help me?"
> Oct. 30, 1922.

We realize your great longing to live only the religious life and that, as you say, you care for nothing that does not bring you closer to the Master Jesus. But, dear student, you forget that everything should thus bring you closer. The difficulties and the conflicting forces which seem to hold you are but the stones in the road. And if we are not strong enough to realize that it is the road, even tho it may be stony and the ruts may seem to be sharp and cutting, then we have not reached the true realization of what life is meant to teach us.

You say your husband, your children and all the conditions of your household keep you back. Instead of this they should be but duties which you gladly do, knowing that every duty well done is a step closer. To keep this always in your mind make up some little sentence which you can repeat over and over with this thought in it, that *nothing* can hold you back; that, everything that seems to keep you back is but something to overcome; that you are not intended to live a life of mere ideal meditation, for you have outgrown this, having lived it in the past; that the Lord Christ knows you are capable of something greater and more important to do for His sake.

Therefore you are given this path to climb up the mountain and you may find many stones and ruts and difficulties in the way, but you should love these difficulties. Say to yourself, "They are not only mine—my husband, my children, my home—but they also belong to the loving Master Jesus. And I can only reach Him when I accept the gifts He gives me and learn to love them and to look upon them as absolutely necessary duties to be accomplished before I can come close to Him. I must walk patiently the Path of Life which He has set for my feet and I must learn to dwell close to Him by doing every duty." Remember there is no obstacle which would push you away more surely than the thought that anything in the world has the power to separate you from this great and loving Friend whom you seek to serve and to love. Build this thought not only in your mind, but also into your sub-conscious mind, so that it shall permeate and fill every atom of your flesh. If performed thus, as service for Him, you will soon enjoy them.

There is a little prayer which is helping many of our pupils; "O Lord Christ, open the door of my body to perfect health. O Lord Christ, open the door of my mind to perfect understanding. O Lord Christ, open the door of my heart to perfect spiritual realization." Say this again and again until your sub-conscious mind knows it and says it even without your volition and builds it into your consciousness and into your flesh.

Also try to conquer fear, and you will when you once let this great thought that the Lord Christ will open the door of your body, mind and heart. And as this door is opened all the love and wisdom and helpfulness will pour in and fill you. Once make your subconscious mind know this and it will never stop building it in, drawing on it like an inexhaustible stream and making you that which you desire to become. Therefore do not grow discouraged. Keep at it constantly. Whenever you feel discouraged, afraid or in any way too tired to think, stop thinking and instead of thinking just repeat these few words. Keep on with them and you will soon find it stops thoughts and fills you with a rest and understanding that your Christ is with you and that you are growing closer to Him.

> "I seem to grow no fruit, 'nothing but leaves.'
> What is the thing that holds me back?"

If you feel that heretofore you have brought forth only leaves, remember the leaves must come first and the fruit must follow. The tree must show its true vigorous growth by putting forth leaves that are healthy, enduring and full of sap.

The fact that you have thus been able to put forth leaves and have awakened to the fact that the time of fruitage is here proves it is possible for you to do better. Therefore ask earnestly in the Silence that you may be shown within yourself just what buds are ready to be pushed to the opening. Very often we have within us great possibilities—let us call them fruit buds—but they are overlaid with a certain selfish or ambitious desire to do something which the world will recognize and admire. And then we push out more leaves, for the things the world sees are leaves. Those who want the fruit must seek deeper for it. Also in putting forth fruit we will often find that which seemed so beautiful for the world is apt to wither. Then truly we begin the struggle.

So, dear student, we say to you, look earnestly within and know absolutely that you not only have these buds which can unfold into fruit, but that you also have the wonderful Divine Helpers waiting only for you to put forth the effort, so that They may crown that effort with success. But you yourself must make the effort. You yourself must find the possibilities and also what it is in you which holds them back.

> "There is so much depression for which I can see no tangible reason. I feel old and still and heavy. By super-human efforts I suppress it for a day or two, but it bobs up again. How am I to overcome it?"
>
> April 4, 1922.

As to the depression you complain of, do not think that you must fight it or suppress it. The thing we fight we strengthen, for we concentrate upon it and it always fights back. This is the natural law of reaction. Instead, find out if possible if there is anything wrong physically with your body, as there may be some poisoning caused by bad teeth, or something of that kind, which could easily be remedied. If there is nothing of this sort to be remedied, then try to live above the condition. Simply realize that the Real you is not old and stiff and heavy, and that your mind is young and light and joyful, and as much as possible through reading and thinking along the lines of the higher truths, come into touch with beautiful things. But if your poor old body insists on being heard, pay as little attention to it as possible. However, remember that before you can ignore it you must give it wise attention. But as we said before, try not to fight the condition or to dwell on it. Use our *Healing Prayer*, then say: "I am not this body. I am a free Soul, and I will dwell with my Christ in the eternal joy of the higher life."

> "You have helped me very much and I am overflowing with thankfulness to you, to the Teacher, to God—for being your pupil. Now that I am out of my former depression I hope to practice much of your instruction and to radiate the happiness it gives."
>
> July 14, 1922.

We are very glad that you have emerged from the cloud of despondency under which you were suffering, and that you have come out into the daylight.

Everyone's life is made up of days and nights. We know that the Sun is always shining even though it passes around to the other side of the world and gives us a night of darkness. But it is sure to come back. And so it is with the Sun of Righteousness. And though we may have our moments of despondency, while it is dark and the Sun of Righteousness does not seem to shine upon us and when all the little personal conditions seem to loom so darkly, yet we know that the day will come.

We feel sure that you are on the right track and will find the answer to most of your troubles if you enter into your own inner Divine Self and there truly ask of God. We know God is everywhere, a mighty friend of Love and Wisdom, but yet when we want to ask of Him we must find Him in our own inner Divine Self. There we will find just as much of God as we have been able to make room for. It is this inner part, or reflection of God, which gives us the assurance of the Truth of all that we want to know. And although it is well to study and to ask of those whom we think perhaps know more than we do, yet even then the ultimate answer to all questions must be given by this God Within before we fully accept it.

> "Is it selfish of me to take the rest and change I am now getting after so long a strain? With it I think I can be of greater assistance to my husband, and I owe it to myself."
>
> Oct. 10, 1922.

You are quite right in realizing that although we do owe a duty to those we love, nevertheless we owe a duty also to ourselves. And it is an important thing for us to decide just how much of ourselves we can give and just what is necessary to make us capable of continuing in our work and helpfulness. It is the duty of each one of us to strive with all our might for physical health, both in body and in mind. If, however, after all our praying "In the Name of the Living Christ," and using every scientific means to retain health, we find that perfect health is denied, then we must realize that some karmic reason underlies it. And we must endure it until we have worked out the Karma. We must seek to understand what is lacking in our present life, or what we have failed to do in the past, and try to correct it.

Never permit yourself to grow discouraged. Realize that perfect health of mind, and the love and understanding of your close touch with the Christ-powers, the desire to be a co-worker with all that this New Age calls for, comes first; that if you are doing your best you can afford to wait, even though the waiting might mean another incarnation. However, never let your mind dwell on this thought. Go ahead as tho the victory was assured you. Have faith, and rest in the love of the Christ.

You can use the *Protecting Invocation* both for yourself and your husband, but altho you might try to interest him in the Teachings, do not overdo it. Stand aside and let it grow. Plant the seed and commend it to the Great Gardener of Souls to till and bring forth in due season. Some people have more in them to hinder the growth of such spiritual seed than do others, just as some soil is more barren and it takes longer for seeds to grow that it does in other soil.

> "I sometimes think it is my varied life that keeps me down. It is hard to understand why one who lives the life I do could be down. Although I do make many mistakes I live close to spiritual understanding."
>
> May 11, 1922.

There is nothing which can really keep a Soul down. Therefore it is not wise to say that it is either your varied life or anything else which is holding you back, for everything sent to us comes to help us. And the Soul which can manifest and come into touch with the Divine in spite of the trials and tribulations we all seem to be destined to cope with, will some day find it has risen higher than those perhaps who have had everything as they wished. It is not those who simply float on the stream of life who awaken in themselves this great love and eagerness and the determination which overcomes difficulties; it is those who find in life things which are hard to conquer. So simply say to yourself that nothing can keep you down. We may suffer poverty; we may find little time to study or do the work we have undertaken for the Master; but if we determine that we will do it in spite of all, and if we have absolute trust that every obstacle we meet is but one more opportunity to grow strong, then we know that we, our Real Self, is not kept down.

This is the attitude of mind you must cultivate. We all make mistakes, but the mistakes which are conquered in the name of the Christ become the stepping stones which lead us up, not down. We are sure that if you have seriously chosen to devote your life to this beautiful work nothing can hold you down; that you will find that every hampering condition will but make you stronger and more determined in the overcoming of life's conditions. One who is filled with this Spirit can never fail. It is only the indifference or rebellion of our lower self that keeps our Higher Self from manifesting, for no matter how buoyant the Spirit in us may be to help us float upward, if we do not follow its guidance it cannot manifest.

> "I have been passing through many experiences and very intense interior life, combined with great material difficulties. I am accepting with gratitude all that the Lord sends me as the means through which I shall acquire wisdom and compassion to become a more efficient worker."
> June 16, 1923.

If we are sincerely trying to bear our personal troubles; trying to send out only love and cheerfulness to others that they may also recognize that they are indeed the children of our Father-in-heaven, then we are really accomplishing great work, And when we are ready to do more, conditions will open in such a way that it will be impossible to fail in this greater work.

Indeed, just that which you describe as your effort toward the higher life is one of the most difficult lessons we have to learn. It is easy to do the big work once we have gained the power; but to grind along day by day, bearing ills which seem so trifling that it seems scarcely worth while to mention them, yet which we find so difficult to bear; still holding fast to the thought that we are God's children; that He does love us with a great and wonderful love; longing that others shall know of this great love—this is our difficult training. But remember that no such effort or desire ever fails to bring its reward. The main reason so many of us seem to be held in the grip of just such sordid surroundings for such a long time is not because we are not ready in many ways for a greater work, but because we need just this understanding that we may teach it to others. Therefore, we who are willing to do that which our Father-in-heaven needs done the most are willing to bear this grinding condition knowing that by so doing we are preparing to help many of His little ones who are not yet ready for a greater work so that they may more understandingly bear the conditions of life which are confronting them. Try to remember this and instead of permitting yourself to become discouraged or lose your hope and trust and love, send it out in greater abundance, and know that no effort is in vain.

Do not be impatient or particularly disturbed by the conditions in the world. They could not disturb us if we truly realized that they are all working upward toward ultimate peace and harmony and love; that it is only when man refuses to let the Light shine in him that this inharmony and violence manifest; that through the very violence and inharmony man suffers from he will ultimately find the peace and love that is being sent to him.

We do not consider you poor, especially spiritually. You are rich in blessings, and if there were more who could pour out the richness of the blessings of their Christ-power, it would help the Order quite as much as the riches of the world. And yet of course during the period through which we are passing, these worldly affairs are of very great and pressing necessity. But we have absolute faith that the Lord of Life understands and will see to it that in time all will come right; and you must have the same faith.

Chapter XIV

JESUS AND THE CHRIST

"In your *Message of Aquaria* you teach that a direct Avatar is never born of mortal woman. Is the orthodox teaching regarding the birth of Jesus an out and out misconception? And how did Mary, the daughter of St. Anne, come to have that honor?"
May 23, 1923.

As to the question regarding the story of Jesus being an out-and-out misconception, *it is by no means such.* The whole history of Jesus, while not a literal history of outer happenings, is the most marvelous teaching, symbolically expressed, of the events of the inner life of every Soul who is on the Path of spiritual evolution. It is therefore far more true than any history of outer events could possibly be; for as is well known, historians make many mistakes in the recording of outer happenings, but the inner mystic symbology of the life of the advancing Soul is so inspirationally given that it is *universally true.* The proof of this is that every Avatar, in the mystic, symbolic presentation of His life, passed through practically the same events, and it would plainly be impossible for a number of Great Teachers to live physical lives on Earth which would absolutely agree in all outer particulars.

Mary, the daughter of St. Anne, as you call her, is a mystic symbol of the great Divine Mother through whom alone the Christ must always be brought forth in the heart of everyone. Joseph symbolizes the intellect, which is not literally the father of the Christ-consciousness, but always stands as the father of the mystic birth in the human Soul. That is, the heart brings forth and the intellect accepts the truth and protects and fathers it before the world.

> "I am mixed up about the Christ and the Christ-force. I cannot pray to a force, but I could to a person who controls that force."
> Oct. 25, 1922.

The Christ is the life aspect of the Godhead, or the Son of God, that which is personalized into a human presentation, as Jesus, who has dwelt on Earth and will dwell on Earth again, yet is always God.

The Christ-force is the emanation of this divine Christ-principle, which expresses itself through creative power in all the universe. Let us compare it with the Sun, which is an orb in the heavens. The Sunforce is the power of the sunlight in all Nature and in all things. Try to make this comparison and realize that the Sun is to Nature what the Christ is to mankind; that its force, which brings forth life and health and growth, works through Nature as does the Christforce in man. In other words, the Sun-force is an aspect of the Christ-force manifesting in Nature.

We do not have to pray to a force, but we do have to contact it through aspiration and let the forces or the emanations of the Divine fill us and draw us closer to it. Perhaps we can understand it better if we think of any human being we know: it is not the person himself who attracts or repels us, but the force he emanates. If the person is evil, his evil thoughts and evil actions make a certain force which repels us and we say we do not like that person. We may not know why, but we do not like him. In other words, his force affects us in a distressing way. But if the person is one who helps us, who sends us loving thoughts and whose whole disposition is radiant with love and helpfulness, we say we like that person and he helps us whenever he comes near us. Now, the Christ-force is just the same, only far greater, more Divine and more wonderful. In fact, it is Divine Life. We are literally within the aura of this mighty loving Son of God. And if we let the radiating force of the Christ permeate us we cannot help but realize more and more the great love and force and helpfulness that is being sent through us. It truly becomes within us living powers which bring forth after their kind. To love the Christ we must let His force manifest through us.

> "I do not understand your teaching: of the Divinity within ourselves and the relation of Jesus to the Christ within as."
>
> July 11, 1923.

The only way we can perhaps simplify the teaching is this: recognize that first you have a body of flesh built up of the atoms which have come to you from the earth, from your parents and from the thought-forces which perhaps you have left behind you in past incarnations, or that have been embodied by your mother during pregnancy. This body is but an evolving physical house which an immortal Divine Soul comes down and inhabits. Now it is this Divine Inner Self which is the Divinity within you, for this Divine Self has come direct from God, is one with God, is Divine. As the *Bible* plainly teaches: "The first man is of the earth, earthy; the second man is the Lord from heaven . . . . And as we have borne the image of the earthy, we shall also bear the image of the heavenly."[1]

The Divine Man finds difficulty, however, in making its divinity shine through, because you and many

---

[1] *I Cor.* XV, 47-9.

many others have permitted yourselves to think that this physical house in which the Soul dwells is you. And quite naturally you cannot find any Divinity in it, as it is not Divine, but physical and mortal. Yet it is the covering and must be made the temple in which the Divine Self can dwell.

As to the relation Jesus Christ bears to the Christ within us, we differentiate between Jesus and the Christ. Jesus was, let us say, a physical manifestation completely filled and permeated with this Divine Christ-principle which is one with God. The Christ is the life and Soul of everything that God has created; everything within us that is Divine; everything in the world. The Christ-spirit (Buddhi) omitting the word Jesus, is the Spirit of all life, the Spirit of all Divinity, the Son and Life-aspect of the Godhead, while Jesus is the personalized manifestation, or the God-man. Therefore the Christ permeates, fills and should dominate all things on the Earth.

The only thing which prevents us from responding to the domination is our own misunderstanding of it and our own thought that the flesh in which this Divine Principle dwells, and perhaps the mind, is all there is of us. This Divine Presence is within us and also with us; it is within, without, around and everywhere. So if we once seek to dwell in the consciousness of the Divine Presence we cannot get away from it.

> "One night I was very lonely, and while praying with closed eyes the form of Jesus came before me with a wonderful love in his face.... Again, when in dire extremity and great danger, I pictured him at my side and He was there as before and the danger went and I was at rest.... Surely this is a surety that He is or was on earth."
> April 5, 1923.

We sincerely appreciate just how you feel as to the presence of Jesus on Earth being absolutely proved because you had a vision of Him. And yet, dear student, you do not seem to understand that Jesus in His life and works and character is always on Earth; that He manifests through many persons, in fact through all who give Him a chance to do so. But since such visions as you saw come from a divine source and with a divine meaning, they are expressed to the one seeing them in the form which will be most impressive. If Jesus represents your highest ideal, then whatever messenger was sent to you would be Jesus in the sense of standing in His place and presenting all His divine attributes. In other words, any messenger from the Divine would naturally take upon himself the conventionalized form you had built up in your mind as representing Jesus, because He must clothe Himself in the highest ideal He finds in your mind.

Therefore, not for the world would we bring any doubt into your mind that your vision was not real. It was real, and it was all that Jesus could be to you, according to your understanding of Him. The only thing we would like to help you to believe is that Jesus appears not to one person, but to many persons, and can appear to all persons who need Him in just the same way. Even if you were a Mohammedan or Buddhist or Hindu you might have the same visitation, and it would seem to you to be either Mohammed or Buddha or Krishna, yet it would be a manifestation of the same Divine Cosmic Christ.

Also the protection and blessing you received from these visions were very real and vivid, and we know they sank deep into your heart and helped to make you one of the pure in heart, knowing well that you had seen God in the habiliments with which your mortal mind had clothed Him. For when He comes to Earth He sends His consciousness, which must always be clothed with the mind stuff of the one receiving the visitation, yet it is always a vision of the Christ.

As to why it should come to you, this we cannot say. Only your own heart knows the eager longing that you perhaps had for the vision, or the great effort you are making to be pure in heart, or the mighty love you were seeking to send out. At any rate, it came to you as a great blessing and as an answer to the earnest prayers you had sent up, whether you realized it or not, for the prayers may have simply welled up out of the depths of your heart without words. We congratulate you and ask you to try always to live up to this vision. Never forget it. And if you are likely to be tempted recall it that it may help you to stay with your feet firmly planted upon the Path.

> "I gather that there was no human disciple named Jesus who was afterwards filled with the Christ Essence; that Jesus the Christ never was a human mortal, hut that He descended and was seen only by those who correlated with Him, as He appeared to the two disciples on the road to Emmaeus. Is that correct?"
>
> Jan. 4, 1923.

Since the very earliest times we find the teachings regarding the Divine Avatar covered up by a simple story of an apparently weak human being who descended into physical life and passed through the various symbolic expressions of human experience and weakness, and was finally seemingly conquered by them. Or we might say, when He has apparently been conquered He has found Wisdom, the Wisdom which alone can make us strong and self-reliant; and has demonstrated this Wisdom by rising above the most ignominious and cruel death.

He thus teaches the Truth to all who can realize

and accept it. He teaches not the literal story as Truth, but the mighty everlasting Truth back of it; not back of the physical history of any one man, but back of all creation, namely, the power of the Soul to pass through the simple every-day occurrences, as a carpenter's son, for instance, and still allow the hidden Divine Wisdom to radiate its helping power to everyone great enough to grasp and understand it. So, in spite of the story of the crucifixion, or any other cruel death through which the many other Avatars are said to have passed, such a death indicated that no miracle can stop the natural results of ignorance and cruelty; only Wisdom and Love filling the hearts of humanity and giving them true understanding can do so.

The mere story of a good man trying to help humanity and suffering persecution and a cruel death, altho it can arouse pity in the hearts of many, can never teach this mighty Truth, unless we take it symbolically and understand deep in our hearts that it is the story of His inner spiritual life—the stages in the unfoldment of the Christ-consciousness, as symbolized by the outer events—that we must follow; that is, the inner mystical understanding of that God-wisdom and God-love which is the answer to all life's mysteries.

The God of Life and Love could never under any circumstances bring to mankind still fiercer persecution and hatred—instead of love and wisdom—directed against those (Jews) who are represented as persecuting the divine revelation of the Christ. But if we refuse to understand or if we are blinded by the surface and literal interpretation of these stories of persecution and cruel death of Those who have come to the world only to bless and uplift humanity, we only help to increase the materialism which has helped to sink the world deeper and deeper in the mire of unwisdom and unbelief. For only Wisdom and Love, which is the Godhead, can bring us out of all this unbrotherliness and persecution and the ignorance which is the cause of it all.

We cannot blame God for our own ignorance. But if we look deeply for the cause of the ignorance we will see that it all comes from the one fact, namely, that certain persons—fallible mortals like ourselves—have in various church councils decided that nothing but a literal interpretation shall be taught. Instead of teaching the great lesson of Love and Wisdom they have tried to force the literal story upon mankind through even worse persecution and greater antagonism. And yet, dear student, can you not grasp the secret of why we are told that only Truth can make us free? When we go back of man's surface explanations of these truths and find the Truth of God, and have lifted up their hearts to Him who is all Truth, then we are free at once from all this miserable agony of indecision and strife which has been the result of accepting truth as man has taught it, rather than looking behind the curtain of ignorance and materialism and finding the spiritual Truth.

According to certain mental science teachings of today, Jesus is regarded as having been less "advanced" than modern teachers in having been weak enough to give way to tears at Lazarus's tomb[2] and as having failed to "demonstrate" over antagonism, persecution, betrayal and death. This is a quite natural deduction if die story is taken literally, and it illustrates the absurd dilemmas into which such literal interpretations place us. In fact, if the spiritual interpretation alone had been taught by the church there would have been none of the persecution and bloodshed—such as the Inquisition, religious wars, etc.—which have resulted from it.

---

[2] *St. John* XI, 35.

You are quite right in saying that if we permit human misconception to condemn Divine Understanding of the Christ, then indeed it is our human intellect which has built, not only a veil, but a strong high wall which shuts out that higher knowledge which is our birthright, namely, the direct inner knowledge of the Divine. But if we believe in this knowledge of the Divine we will soon find it demonstrated to us in a most marvelous way. As you know, we can appeal to our higher Divine Self, and if we do this without fear, without holding falteringly to the hand of human understanding lest we be damned (not by God, for He never damned anything, but by the wall of human ignorance, mistakes, etc.), then we will soon get our answer, and this answer will be a convincing one.

> "If Jesus was the Savior of mankind, why should He have remained so short a time on Earth and why was He permitted to be crucified?"
> July 19, 1922.

This would be a very natural question if you take the story of Jesus the Christ literally as it is given in the *Bible*. If He was, as you say, a Divine Being, the Son of God, which indeed He was, then having no Karma, why should He suffer so much or why should His loving Father demand a blood sacrifice of His only beloved Son for the sins of the world?

According to our Teachings, instead of taking these stories literally and as historical facts, we must take them as we take all other religious teaching, *i.e.*, simply as allegorical representations of divine spiritual truths. When we do this we find that the Lord Christ or the Christ-consciousness dwells in each heart. And it is in these hearts or these human manifestations that He comes and suffers and is crucified by our failure to recognize and follow His guidance. Only as we recognize that He thus suffers in us and for us (and the suffering is very real and true) can we learn to lift up the cross on which He is crucified and hail Him as the Son of God seated forever more at the right hand of the Father, striving to lead us through Divine Love into the path of blessedness; no longer to suffer and die, but to live forevermore both in us and in the world.

Therefore, instead of bemoaning the supposedly cruel death which is said to have happened to a human representation of our God many hundreds of years ago, we must look within ourselves and realize that this same Christ our Lord is still manifesting on the Earth, is going up and down the city (our body) teaching and seeking to draw us and all our faculties to a fuller and higher understanding of God's truth. We must know that whenever we turn away from this inner guidance we are crying out, "Crucify him. Crucify him"; that by this crucifixion He suffers until we as individuals accept and lift Him up in our consciousness as the Son of God and let Him shine in our hearts and reign in our lives. Then as we help the whole world to live in the Light of this Love, the crucifixion will be over forevermore.

> "I would like to know the truth about the origin of the Christ (Jesus) as a being and His relative position to humanity as a Savior. . . . Was He ever a man who erred as humanity errs and who gained Mastery and then Divinity? . . . I feel the need of a clear and full knowledge of the Christ, for my heart warms at the thought and I feel that I love Him, but love wants to know of its Beloved more and more."
>
> Dec. 7, 1922.

The story of Jesus, like the stories of all great Avatars, is but a mythical portrayal of the steps through which every human being on the Path to Mastery must pass. When we say mythical we do not mean that there never was such a being as Jesus, for there was and He was a great Master of Masters. He was indeed an Avatar, not simply one after His baptism, as taught by some, but from His very descent to Earth.

Jesus the Christ as the Savior of humanity is the same great Avatar in His universal aspect as the Light and Life and Son of His Father, manifesting through this world, through all creatures and all things as that Power which is forever drawing them upward and Godward. Therefore, in one sense the two are one. Yet as Jesus He seems to come closer to us, because Jesus was the human aspect in which He manifested. If we recognize that in reality the Christ manifests through the Higher Self of each Soul passing through its pilgrimage of Earth and lifting up all the events of Earth, then in very truth He is closer and we can call on Him to enter into us and help us to pass through all our trials.

We are apt to call Jesus a man "like unto ourselves," but as we have said, the story is mythical and is a symbolic outpicturing of every event in spiritual evolution, hence "like unto ourselves." We must never separate Him from the Christ, yet it must always be the Christ whom we are serving.

It is indeed a reappearance or, let us say, reembodiment of this same Avatar whom we now expect. We wish we could make this so plain that there would be no danger of misunderstanding, but it is difficult. For by embodiment we do not mean that this Great One whom we call Jesus the Christ will be born as a physical babe, but that He will descend, as do all Divine Avatars, from His Father-in-heaven and manifest phenomenally in human form to all who can recognize Him. He may be called by some Krishna or Buddha or Maitriya or any other name which stands in certain countries and religions for the idea we are seeking to explain. But it will be the same principle, the Divine Life-aspect of the Father, the same outpouring of Divinity, which is to descend to humanity just as soon as the reaping is over and the elect have been gathered together and are ready to receive Him.

He is our Savior in that only through the inflowing of the Divine Life-force of the Christ can the human personality be saved from becoming a mere intellectual animal, and the body be purified by the sublimation of all its inharmonies, diseases, sins and imperfections, that it may become a fit Temple of the Living God, the immortal Soul of man.

As to gaining a full and clear knowledge of the Christ, this you can do, dear brother, but the way to do it is to seek Him in your heart. And when it warms at the thought and you feel that great love filling you, say to yourself, "This is true. This very love that is in me is the outpouring of His heart, and I can draw close to Him only through love. I can know and will know my Beloved more and more only as I seek for Him within myself and also in my brothers and sisters; only as I try to live true, to watch for Truth, to take no subterfuge, to listen to words of love which come in His messages to mankind; only as I refuse to take as His anything that does not measure up to this divine outpouring of Christ-light in the world."

> "From your explanation of the crucifixion am I to infer that you deny the actuality of the event from a human and historical standpoint?"
> Jan. 4, 1923.

We do say most emphatically that the crucifixion is an allegory, not an historical and physical event, for there is no record of such an event in contemporaneous history. Yet when the great Avatar or the Son of God did descend to Earth He quite naturally did have a more or less personal experience here, altho the *Bible* story is not a record of that experience, hut of the spiritual experience which the story symbolizes. For when the Godhead takes upon itself perfected human expression it becomes human in but a very limited way, for there are certain phases which Divinity can no longer enter into. It cannot descend into the lower aspects of human creation and be born as a mortal babe, but manifests phenomenally to mankind to teach and uplift all who will listen and follow; then the manifestation passes away, leaving a great stream of Light which can be comprehended by those whose minds are illumined by it or respond to it.

> "Some teach that when Jesus was baptized the Christ descended and occupied Jesus' perfected body for His three years ministry. Are Christ and Jesus separate individuals? . . . . Why are your prayers addressed to Christ and not to God?"
> Dec. 9, 1922.

We do not at all agree with what we know is the . . . . teaching, namely, that at Jesus' baptism the Christ descended and occupied a perfected human body.

This whole problem is largely explained in our *Message of Aquaria* in a number of chapters, and also in Chapter X of our *Voice of Isis*, and Chapter VII of *The Key of Destiny*. Jesus the man represents humanity in all its phases of spiritual unfoldment; the Christ is the universal Christos or divine cosmic outshining of the Father which descends to Earth at stated intervals and is personalized in a divine Avatar, one who is not a mortal, never has been a mortal and who has practically no personal history at all. It is a miraculous appearance on Earth. He gives His Teachings and appears to those to whom He chooses to appear, but is unknown and unnoticed by others. Such an outshining of the Christ, or let us say, descent of the Christ-light—in a superhuman divine body—is now expected just as soon as this awful cleaning up of the old Karma of the world is accomplished.

Naturally if you take this view, you will see that the story of the Christ entering the man Jesus at the moment of His baptism symbolizes that when humanity reaches such a point, this great divine Christ Consciousness enters into it. And today humanity must prepare for its baptism in the Jordan,[3] or its spiritual enlightenment. We would gladly help you to understand this, for indeed it is one of the greatest problems for the world to solve; one that the materialism of the church's teaching has helped to make more dense through the past ages. That is why we say that each one who touches this Christ-light in his heart will know Him when He comes. He will come in a human form, but it will be a phenomenal appearance. He will not be born of woman.

As to your description of what you believe to be the Christ, it is very close to the Truth, altho the Christ is more than merely a principle of love. It is love and life and redemption and glorification. It will not only descend to Earth and touch with its own radiant garment all who are purified enough to recognize this Christ-light and accept it, but it will also help to rehabilitate this dark world after its purification, which is even now upon us. Therefore, you are quite right in saying that the only way we can come to the Father is through this Christ Consciousness, for no one can have any real conception of God until the Light of the Christos has manifested within him.

---

[3] See *The Message of Aquaria*, Curtiss, chapters XXVII-VIII.

As to our prayers and affirmations being addressed to Christ rather than to God, Christ and God are one, but Christ, the Christos, is the outshining of God which touches Earth. It is just as we might tell an invalid to go and sit in the sunshine. We would not say go sit in the Sun, but we would tell him to sit where the Sun shines. So the Christos is the spiritual sunshine, just as surely a part of the Father as the shining of the Sun is part of the Sun. But it is that part which touches the Earth and enters into your physical consciousness and lifts you up in the divine consciousness where you become one with God.

> "If the life of Jesus is but a universal allegory of the stages of manifestation of the Christ Consciousness in the unfolding of each Soul, what hope have we that He will soon manifest again?"
> April 17, 1923.

According to our Teachings, Jesus Christ Himself is a great Avatar, the Son of God. All such come to the world at stated times and give to the world Their blessing and Their Teachings, but we might say in one sense that They have no personal history at all. Now, altho this may perhaps seem to you difficult to understand, nevertheless it is corroborated in the *Bible* when we are told that Jesus Christ was an example[4] for humanity. Therefore when we are trying to make His almost mystical and marvelous life on Earth understandable to the many, it must be given forth in a mystical way. For all such manifestations of Divinity who touch the Earth—and it is always a manifestation of the same cosmic Christ-power—have no personal life whatever, because to become such a great Divine outpouring of the Godhead means to have overcome all

---

[4] *I Cor.* X, 11. *Galatians* IV, 22-4.

personality: not to be held fast to personality in any way whatever.

Therefore the only way the Earth manifestation of such a Divine Personage could possibly be told to human beings would be in a more or less allegorical manner. And if you notice carefully you will find that every event in His life corresponds absolutely with the inner spiritual life of every Soul on Earth. In other words, because the Christ is the life-force of humanity and abides not only in one, but in all, when we get down to the understanding of this life-force we find that it always manifests in the same way. It always has to confront and fight with the earthly conception; always has to be crucified; to atone for the personality; and we can never overcome our personal ideas until we have literally hung on the cross of matter or suffered in the flesh: not what you would call a literal cross to which you are nailed, but nevertheless a cross of matter wherein all that is most holy and Divine is apparently put to death. Yet it ultimately rises from the dead and conquers in you and ultimately in the whole world.

We know this is difficult to grasp and understand, especially in the light of the many ages of personalization and materialization of this story, yet what we tell you is true. If it is not true to you and if you find more help and comfort in believing in the old orthodox literal interpretation of the Gospels, by all means take what comfort you can and try to live this Christ-life to the best of your ability. For we know well that when any Soul has honestly and sincerely tried to draw close to the Christ, that Soul finds Him, not in the personality of a man crucified ages ago, but within himself, a very spark of Divinity and oneness with the Father.

So as long as it seems to you to be simply hairsplitting and unsatisfactory, lay it aside and wait. God never expects any of His children to believe or to do that which to them at their stage of development seems impossible. He knows well that we are but children and that we will grow both in understanding and in love and in appreciation of the Christ. We have all eternity to grow in, for we are told most positively that Jesus the Christ is the same yesterday, today and forever.

> "I appreciate your teachings immensely, but I had the temerity to associate my life with the Bible. Most of the events of Jesus' life seemingly have happened to me. How do you explain this?"
> Aug. 24, 1924.

The reason that your life appears to be wrapped up with the life of Jesus, and hence fits in with all the allusions and prophecies pertaining to it, is firstly because you are growing in spirit closer and closer to Him and hence identify yourself more and more with your ideal of Him. And, secondly, because you had an incarnation during the early Christian era and were identified with the early apostolic teachers. During that time your mind was so saturated with the great love of the Christ, and you believed so implicitly in the truth of what the early Christians called reality, that those ideas were impressed upon your Soul-consciousness as Truth, hence you bring over the strong impression of a personal realization of it all.

In the very early days of the Christian church, before any set creed and dogmas were formed and imposed upon its followers, the teachers and leaders understood the mystery of the Divine Manifestation which had taken place and hence called real all things that were inner and of the Soul, all the mystical experiences and realizations, etc. While they naturally understood that the Gospel story—which took nearly a hundred years to elaborate and put into its present set form—did not refer to, physical and historical events, but to spiritual events. Nevertheless they knew it was everlastingly true and a great reality in the spiritual life. Realizing that spiritual things must be spiritually discerned they were quite justified in teaching it as true, for no one was expected to take it materialistically and literally, but symbolically and allegorically. It was only as the Gnostics, the "Knowers," were persecuted and the inner teachings driven out by the materialism of succeeding centuries that the true interpretation was lost and the literal gradually taught.

Indeed this inner, mystical teaching was the cause of most of the martyrdoms and persecutions of the early Christians, for they insisted upon the reality of the Gospel story without being able to explain what they meant by reality. And as, even in those early days, no historical data could be found to substantiate their claims of reality, they were persecuted as a dangerous and misleading sect.

Those early followers could not explain to an ignorant world that the story of Jesus was never meant to be taken literally as the later and present-day Christians have taken it. And yet it was truly His story, an outpicturing of His life and experiences of Earth in its mystical sense or spiritual interpretation in connection with His work as one with the triune Godhead or God-with-us, Emanuel. While it is His real life story, it is the mystical and allegorical history of His inner, hence absolutely true, spiritual life.

For this reason the story of every Divine Savior of mankind, in every age and in every religion, and known by whatever name He may be called, is practically the same—the same main events in the same sequence. (Look this up in our *Key of Destiny*, Chapters vi and vii. Also look up every reference to the word Avatar in all our books.)

Since this marvelous story is the history of the unfolding and manifesting of the Christ-consciousness in every heart after the Christ-seed has begun to sprout, every human being who is drawn very close to this Divine Inner Christ, according to his love and devotion, finds the same events seeming to be his own. And because of the insistence of the church upon such a material interpretation such persons have thought it a physical event. And since they have given themselves to Jesus and prayed to do His work on Earth, they have embodied these events and reproduced them in their own consciousness, just as all ideas held to strongly reproduce their effects in our lives and even in our bodies.

Try, dear brother, to realize that this is one of the greatest mysteries, as well as one of the most tremendous truths in the universe, altho historically it is but an allegory, as we have tried so hard to explain in our lessons and books. Quite naturally, since Jesus is the Sun of God, He is shedding His Light direct into the heart of humanity, just as the physical Sun in the heavens is destined to shed its life-giving force (blood) into the heart of the Earth and all it produces, as long as the Earth shall endure.

Now, here you must put forth all the power of your intellect to understand and all your intuition to illumine this paradox. Jesus, the Sun of God and the destined Illuminator and Savior of mankind—as the Sun is the illuminator and savior of all physical life on Earth—can never, and never could under any circumstances, transfer His work to another, be that one an Angel or God, any more than the physical Sun can transfer its work—which to the Earth is of the same nature as that of the Son to mankind—to another planet.

With this understanding, and the realization that Jesus is not and never was a mortal, in your inner self you can say that you are one with the Christ, as all men must be some day. And that you are chosen, as many, many others, to do the work of Jesus to the extent that they can let the Light of the Christ shine out through them into the world. It is therefore a pleasure to help you to understand your work; for you have passed many incarnations in trying to do it, but always more or less hampered by your misunderstanding of the story. In this life you now have the opportunity to get this misconception straightened out and accomplish so much more.

> "You write: 'No one who is seeking Spiritual Truth in earnest, in humility and sincerity is making a mistake. We must first seek it mentally, or at least some of us do so, but it is always born in the heart. And only when the heart stands as its mother (Mary) to give birth to the spiritual consciousness of that Truth, can the intellect (Joseph) stand before the world as its father, although this child of spiritual understanding has really been fathered by the overshadowing of the Most High, the Spirit of Truth.' Do you really mean this?"

July 24, 1922.

As to what we mean by first seeking Truth mentally, first your mind must grasp the fact that there is something you want to know. But it is a long time before your mind realizes that the real Truth you are seeking is born in your heart. And when it is born in your heart, besides the mere desire to know and to understand born in your mind, there comes a realization that all you are seeking is true. That is what we mean by being "born in your heart." Then the realization that is thus born must be carefully nurtured, not pushed aside and denied the nourishing forces which will give it life, but really taken care of so that it will grow and become the living Christ who shall fill all your being. Then indeed the mind, which before but vaguely sought and groped for Truth, steps forward and makes it his child or fathers this newborn ideal, because the mind recognizes that to which the heart has given birth and admits it to his fatherly care and nourishing. "That which is born of the flesh is flesh, and that which is born of the Spirit is Spirit."

Only when the mind is straightened out and says, "I am willing to learn," will the truth and the Christ-child be born in the heart; and only after its birth will the mind recognize it and father it. First the mind must recognize and seek, then the heart will bring forth when the time comes. It is true that all earnest, sincere desire to penetrate the mysteries of life is an instinct of the Soul born in us from the heart, or as we tried to put it in the earlier part of this letter, it is our recognition in a vague, mystic way of this great broadcasting of the mystic Wisdom of all ages.

> "I do feel so grateful for the lesson *The Lord Jesus Christ*, for I, perhaps like many others, am inclined to look too much at and to the personality of Jesus instead of to the cosmic Christ-principle which He embodied. . . . If the life of Jesus was merely a manifestation of the allegorical Christ Myth, how could He have actually manifested to man? If the Christ is only a divine experience in every Soul and the incidents related in the Bible are not historical, how could He have had an immaculate birth?"

Aug. 15, 1923.

There are many religious in the world, every one of them founded upon the words and the teachings of some manifestation of the Cosmic Christ, yet only the Christians call it the Christ. The Christ therefore manifests under various names, but the point we wish to emphasize is that this everlasting Divine Life-power which emanates from the Godhead is everywhere and is the substance of religion wherever religion is found. Nor is there a human being who has not felt in some form or other this everlasting Power drawing him to something higher and above this mundane sphere. What we call the Christ is this outpouring of Divine Life, Love and Wisdom which is expressed in the story of Jesus the Christ.

It matters not whether we belong to any so-called religion; as long as we recognize this force and power we are in truth worshiping the Christ. Some call it Christ, some Krishna, some Buddha, etc. Yet all represent the same underlying cosmic principle or ideal. And to be true to this universal ideal and seek to let it manifest in your life is the only true religion. The name by which we call it matters not: just as all humanity are God's children and it matters not whether, we call them John or Harry or any other name.

As to the accounts of His life, these in the Christian religion, as well as in all other religions, are both racial and mythical, *i.e.*, each race expresses the ideal story to the best of its ability. Yet when we study the life in its spiritual aspect we will find that its underlying ideas are all the same or very similar. Each is expressing the Divine Emanation of the Godhead and Its manifestation to man according to its highest understanding of what God should be to man.

All are immaculately born of Mary, the Divine Mother, or in the heart, and all pass through the various experiences through which Jesus passed symbolically. In this world of unbelief and antagonism all are crucified or meet with some cruel death, then return to manifest to their disciples and finally ascend to their Father and sit at the right hand of God, sending down to Earth their power of sustenance and love and help to all His children that these children may grow closer and closer to Him. If the whole world were able to speak one language and think as one man then we might find them able to express this mighty and wonderful ideal of God in the same way.

Therefore, we should never call "heathen" those who differ from us in worship, for they are worshipping their highest conception of God as are we, perhaps more sincerely and devotedly than we.

The word immaculate does not mean, as so many think, to be born without a father. It means pure, unmixed. And if we could enter into the consciousness of every Soul who is trying to express this divine ideal which we call Christhood, we would find that this ideal is born immaculately in the heart, unmixed with any other thought: that all the explanations put upon it are but the overlying personalized allegory, let us call it, which clothes this inner spiritual event; just as the personality of every human being, composed of earth particles and mental conceptions, overlies the Divine Soul that is striving to manifest through that personality.

Therefore, while Jesus is represented as fulfilling all the incidents of the cosmic Sun Myth, He is more than a myth. He is its exemplifier. And while He comes personally to each heart He also manifests phenomenally, in the way we have described elsewhere,[5] to His chosen Disciples wherever and whenever and to the extent that they make the necessary conditions.

---

[5] See *The Voice of Isis*, Curtiss, Chapter X. *The Message of Aquaria*, Curtiss, Chapters XIX, XX, XXII, XXXV to XXXVIII.

Chapter XV

MISCELLANEOUS

"If we have a just God, why is the forgiveness of sin impossible?"

March 6, 1923.

The forgiveness of sins is not impossible. However, the difference between the forgiveness of sins and the overcoming of sins is great, and little understood, but if once understood we could not believe that any just God would make of sin such a calamity as not to forgive it. All sin is but a mistake, a misconception of a reality, hence it needs not only forgiveness, but also correcting, redeeming and wiping out. And for this we need to understand it. Once we understand how to develop our faculties so as to attain godliness and seek for the Inner Light and permit it to shine through the flesh, then there will be no sin to forgive; for man will have followed his guidance and become like unto Him.

Therefore, the Father is ever ready to forgive our sin or mistake provided we are ready to acknowledge it and try to correct it. But forgiving us for making a mistake does not mean that we will not have to reap its results, for as we sow so shall we reap. If through disobedience a child is burned the parents readily forgive it and love it all the more because of its suffering, but in spite of the forgiveness the child must still suffer the pain of the burn. Once we understand that every event in life is calculated to bring to the mind of him whom, for the sake of understanding, we will call the sinner, the mistakes he has made and the reasons for them, then there is no question of not being forgiven. Through such recognition does man grow; for the whole object of life is for man to understand himself and to know why he makes these mistakes.

The man who sins otherwise than through ignorance is a fool, because the teaching is there for him to follow, and there is forever held out to him the hand of Divine Love which will lead him into perfect understanding and perfect co-ordination with Divine Love and forgiveness. We like to say, instead of forgiving sin, that God is so Divine that He overlooks our foolishness and leads us gently but firmly and unwaveringly through no matter how much suffering ultimately into the Path of Wisdom.

> "This will not be my first acquaintance with mysticism, as I have studied with the .... Society and the ...., but it seems I have not yet found what you call one's true spiritual home. I would like your opinion of young people entering these studies."
>
> Aug. 22, 1923.

The fact of our sending you a letter of welcome into the Order would be in itself an answer, as it would show that we did not consider you too young to take up the studies.

In fact, from our point of view, the younger you begin these studies the better, because it is an indication that you have come into this incarnation with more or less of a memory of past efforts; so the sooner the studies are taken up the better. Had you not studied along the same lines in the past you would not desire such studies at the age of sixteen; and in taking them up at your age there will not now be a long interval in which the affairs of the world enter your consciousness and push back the natural memories and habits of thought and life you had so well learned in the past.

You will find in the Teachings of this Order quite a little that differs in detail from the . . . . explanation, but you will also find that both of us, as well as the . . . . , and almost every other Order that is trying to set forth similar work, are striving under the particular Masters who are leading and guiding these movements, to emphasize certain aspects of the same Wisdom Religion. You are therefore quite right to seek until you decide which is your real true spiritual home; and that will be the special phase of spiritual teaching which seems to explain life to you the most completely and which helps your own particular inner convictions to work outwardly.

The main difference between our form of teaching and that of either of the other societies you name is that they are striving to elucidate the intellectual side of the Mysteries; yet during all the ages that the intellectual side has been emphasized, we do not feel it has touched the deep heart-hunger of those who are seeking not so much for intellectual development as for personal contact with and realization of the Divine, and the loving tender touch with the Divine Hierarchy which can lead them step by step through the devious paths of earth-life and explain each condition they meet.

We claim, therefore, nothing special for our Teachings except we are doing our best to set forth Truth in a little different way, and we leave to our pupils the choice. However, we emphasize very positively the fact that we are trying to give out the inner mystical Teachings of what we consider true World Religion, which embraces all religions, and we are perfectly willing to let the students choose between our way of setting them forth and what we have explained as an intellectual and outer way of explaining matters.

> "I would like an explanation as to which is correct. In one place you speak of the Nirmanakaya, or fire body, and in another, of the Nirmanakaya, or spiritual body. Which is correct?"
>
> July 14, 1922.

As to what is meant by the Nirmanakaya body, it actually means a body of spiritual fire. In reality, as we tread the Path of Discipleship and one by one overcome our faults and failings and draw closer and closer to the Divine Light of the Christos, we literally change the atoms of our bodies from mere atoms of earthly forces into fire atoms. It is not fire in the sense of something that consumes and burns up, but spiritual fire.

As we go on, life after life, conquering and building in these fire atoms, there comes a time in some incarnation when all the atoms of our bodies are thus turned into spiritual fire. Then we are said to put on the Nirmanakaya body, or the fire or spiritual body. In other words, we have redeemed the flesh. But we do not do this all at once. As we have said, it takes many incarnations. However, if we are earnest and sincere and determined, we do, in each life, redeem a certain number of atoms. Then in our next incarnation this number will be built around the sacred centers, until there does come a time when they are all redeemed. When this time comes we are no longer subject to physical death because we are no longer of the earth earthy, but have become the Master of conditions. This fire body is therefore the spiritual body of Mastery and of the perfected Super-man who is clothed with a spiritual body, the atoms of which are spiritual fire.

Miscellaneous

> "Will you please tell me if my supposed Initiation by . . . . was a disaster, or if I have merely been passing through a phase quite necessary. Much depends on the answer I receive. I would also like to know what took place at that time. Was it hypnotism? Was it a true Initiation, or was it an infernal society that works through evil things?"
> April 23, 1923.

It was hardly necessary to tell you who it was who was supposed to give you the Initiation, as we have had so many letters just like yours. We will say only this: that there is no such thing as an Initiation given by a human being which is capable of giving you great spiritual unfoldment or advance, for all true *spiritual initiations* are first given to you in the higher realms with the full understanding of your own Soul, by a Divine Being not on the physical plane, and later work out in the events of your subsequent life. Sometimes after this inner event you pass through a certain ceremony which will be recognized in every one of its stages as that which you have already passed through in your higher Sublime Self. But quite often there is no such ceremony. Life itself works out one by one the questions which have been asked you, and altho you generally have no memory of the answers you gave in your mystic initiation, yet you will always find that events bring to you the same decisions as in your mystic initiation.

As to its being disastrous in your case, it would certainly be so were it real. As to how to break it, we would say that by the power of the Christ you can break it as well as break any influence any mortal might have over you. Repeat daily and hourly "I am a child of the Living God. I have no link with any human being except those who serve the Lord Christ; for these and these alone are my brethren and sisters."

Say to yourself, "No one has any power over me against my will, and my Father-in-heaven will protect me from all that is harmful. Whatever has come to me in the past I am willing to work out, for nothing is disastrous that comes with the sanction of this great love. In the name of the Living Christ, Amen."

As to telling you all that took place at the time you speak of, we refuse even to think of it and we want you to do the same. It is gone, forever gone, swallowed up in the blackness of the evil which seeks to shut out God from your consciousness.

> "You speak of the seed as if the pattern were on the Astral Plane. Is this that we see here the symbol and the true flower on the next plane? Is the Higher Self there, too? Some say the Soul is never in the body."

June 12, 1922.

You are quite right in thinking that there is no sign of the pattern of the tree or flower within the seed. As the seed is planted in the Earth the pattern descends from the higher spiritual realms through the astral. Then as the seed grows, this pattern is gradually materialized in the physical world. That is, the pattern of all things exists in the Divine Realm, and to manifest on Earth it must pass down through all realms, building around the pattern the substance of each particular realm through which it is passing. This is true of the tiniest seed which grows in the Earth and is equally true of the Soul of man which descends to manifest on Earth.

As to the Higher Self being in the body, this is true in a certain sense, but it is a spiritual mystery. Just as the Divine Flame is within the seed which will grow into the pattern which is descending through all the realms, so does the Divine Self—which is a part of Divinity or, we might say, a spark sent out by the

Great Flame we call God—descend through all the realms and become clothed with the substance of each realm. And when it reaches the physical realm, it must enter in and be clothed with the substance of this physical realm. This is why we speak of the Higher Self as being one with God, and yet this Higher Self has within the body of flesh only as much of the Pattern as it has been possible to manifest or to unfold. And for this reason, as long as we identify our consciousness with the physical body and call it the Self, we are not unfolding the true pattern of our Divine Self. If we always realize this Divine Self as seeking to clothe itself with purified atoms, we will gradually grow into the image of our real true Self.

> "Will you kindly explain about the five loaves and the two small fishes?"
>
> Dec. 2, 1922.

The five loaves and the two small fishes symbolize man's five physical senses and his two higher ones. Bread is a fundamental physical food and thus symbolizes the five physical senses which supply the vibrations and experiences which form the fundamental food of man's conscious mental life; for these senses are used on the physical plane to supply the materials of his physical consciousness. But the two higher senses—the two small fishes—must be used to contact the higher planes and feed the spiritual consciousness.

They should also be used to help feed those who are willing to take the trouble to take hold of and use the line that connects them with the Great Deep or the depths of Divine Love and seek to bring up the two fishes or develop their two higher senses. Fish are used for this simile because they swim in the depths of the sea and are not easily seen, altho they can be brought to the surface and utilized for food if the proper methods are used. They symbolize the inner mystical Truth which helps to digest the Bread of Life and make it more satisfying and nourishing.

> "What do your Teachings say about hunting? Today all have gone hunting; they hunt for deer, for coon, wildcat, squirrel, rabbits, etc. I have no inclination to hunt myself. Is it wrong to hunt these and kill them? Is it wrong to kill a snake? If I have any stock sick and infirm, do I do wrong to kill them if I hold the thought that they come back in more perfect bodies? This country is very rugged and the people make little effort to improve or help animals."
>
> Dec. 14, 1922.

As we have said most emphatically in our books and Teachings, hunting for sport is very cruel and wrong and tends to put even greater enmity between man and beast, who should co-operate and be friends. But there are certain times when it is almost necessary to take life, *i.e.*, to kill certain destructive animals, vermin, rodents, wolves, etc., else it will be giving them a supremacy over man, and man must be the ruler of this Earth; must be able to bring forth his crops and not only feed himself but improve the Earth and its increase.

If we simply send such creatures away from our immediate neighborhood, as it is quite possible to do with the mystic powers at our command, we are sending them to prey on others and to continue to interfere with the perfecting of the Earth for man's benefit; for all such destructive pests are but the fulfillment of the curse: "Cursed is the ground for thy sake; in sorrow shalt thou eat of it"; for all such things prey not only on man, but literally curse the increase of the Earth. However, if we take the attitude that as this Earth is especially made to be man's field of experience and to give him his living—because he has become so dense that he can only live and manifest under certain dense conditions—then he must take seriously not only the gifts this Earth can give him but also the responsibilities. And whatever he does he must do in the attitude of mind that that thing is necessary to be done; necessary not only for himself, but for the rest of the world. Thus everything he finds it necessary to kill, he must kill with his blessing, recognizing and knowing that here on this dense planet the animal atoms are ultimately transformed into the human or into the next higher manifestation. In holding this thought strongly, man is perfectly safe, in taking whatever steps are necessary to rid himself and his neighbors of vermin, rodents and destructive creatures.

We can see plainly why there should be so much destructive game in your neighbourhood; your last paragraph explains this. The fact is that the people living there make no effort to improve their stock, but are satisfied with razor-backed hogs, miserable cattle, etc. It is man's duty to improve the animal creation, to lift it up to its highest stage of development so that the atoms composing it may be the more readily transformed into a higher manifestation. Therefore the best thing one person can do in such a neighborhood is to try in every way to teach his neighbours; then to help to send everything which is not the highest of its species into a new stage of evolution. This condition is by no means an ideal one; in fact, there is very little on this planet that is ideal. But it is a necessary condition for us to pass through, as it teaches man quite as much as he, if he is doing his duty, can teach the lower animals.

> "Do we have to meet and overcome the Dweller on the Threshold many times? If so, how can we know when we have fully conquered?"
>
> Aug. 12, 1922.

We meet a different phase of this Dweller at each step on the Path. The Dweller is the composite picture of all our unconquered failings, and as we never conquer them all at once, the Dweller on the Threshold will take on for us the symbolism of the particular phase we have not conquered. This is why it is called the Dweller on the Threshold, for it meets us on the threshold of every new step, and will push us back until conquered.

How you will know when you have fully conquered the Dweller will be when you have really conquered all the special faults that now assail you.

> "In what light does your Order regard the biblical prophecies which some think point to English, Scotch and Irish and their descendants, being the lost tribes of Israel? If so might we not expect a Teacher to come from some family of the House of David from which the British Empire has descended?"
>
> July 7, 1923.

In regard to the biblical prophecies which are taken to apply to the various English-speaking peoples, as you no doubt know from a study of our books and Teachings, we interpret the *Bible*, almost entirely from a symbolical and spiritual standpoint rather than from a literal and materialistic standpoint. For instance, the twelve sons of Jacob refer not to twelve individuals or even twelve definite nations, but to the twelve types of people who are born under the twelve zodiacal signs. There are many other passages which show that the chief personages mentioned in the *Bible* stand for certain principles, qualities, or for types of people, and not definite nations, some of which have arisen thousands of years after the statements or prophecies were given.

Interpreted from this higher and broader standpoint "the chosen people" does not refer to the Hebrew tribes nor to any nation or race, but to all peoples of whatever nation or race who obey the Divine Law, symbolized by Moses the Lawgiver. They become the "chosen" because they have chosen to obey the Law, conquer their personal faults and failings and follow the Divine. From this standpoint a study of history will show that none of the nations you mention can be said to have fulfilled the qualifications of the "chosen people" altho countless individuals among these and still other nations have done so. Therefore, the "lost ten tribes" would be the vast majority of people who do not consciously strive to follow the Divine Law, ten always meaning a complete or vast number. And of all mankind who are born under the twelve signs of the zodiac those who do not follow the Law, and hence are "lost," predominate in the proportion of ten to two. The prophecy which you quote (Gen. 48-49) refers to those few who like Joseph have followed the Law and have therefore been blessed by it (Jacob), and who because they do work in harmony with that Law are promised that ultimately they shall become a multitude and inherit the Earth. For some time in the coming aeons all mankind, after much wandering and suffering "in the wilderness" of the outer life, will be purified and reach true godliness.

The blessing given to the two sons of Joseph indicates that those whom the "chosen ones" bring forth shall all be blessed. That the younger is blessed more than the elder indicates that the later generations of the followers of the Law shall live in ages when they can learn more, have a greater understanding of Divine Law, bring forth greater spiritual results and so receive greater blessings than the races living during more primitive times, altho the latter will be the same people reincarnated. With this interpretation in mind we think you can interpret the other prophecies, such as Isaiah 49:20, etc., and will not limit them to Americans alone. For while the main seat of the New Race is likely to be in America, that New Race will be made up of the highest and best of all races who can work together to serve the Lord or the Divine Law, in peace, harmony and co-operation. Owing to catastrophes, etc., America will then be much larger than at present, hence able to accommodate all who come.

As to the House of David, that will include all who have made Divine Love (symbol of David) their guiding star, altho they also need the lessons of the House of Solomon, or Wisdom, as well. When these are all gathered together they will form one Household of Faith, whether they are all bodily present in America or not.

Inasmuch as certain of the nations you name seem to have literally fulfilled certain prophecies, it means that to that degree those nations have responded to the opportunity to accomplish certain ends, but before the whole can be fulfilled and they become the "chosen people" they must be tried and tested. For only those in such nations who have thus passed the great tests of life can fulfill the spiritual meaning of the prophecy.

> "You touch quite truly on the point of many vegetarians want of tolerance, but there are some other considerations which it seems to me can be looked upon from such an angle that their universal truth and acceptability appears doubtful."
>
> Oct. 22, 1922.

As to the chapter in our *Voice of Isis*, "Thou Shalt Not Kill," this is not a controversial subject, but owing to the fact that we always stand for the middle ground and desire to express both sides of every subject, also the fact that the so-called vegetarians have said so much on their side and there has been so little said on the other side, we felt that the subject was not treated at all fairly unless both sides were set forth, so that each Soul may judge for itself. If you will read carefully, you will see that at the beginning of this chapter we say "This lesson is intended to advocate neither meat-eating nor non-meat-eating, but to inculcate in all that tolerance which can see others follow lines of conduct differing from their own without condemnation or a feeling of superiority." Therefore, there is nothing to controvert, and we will only say that we advocate neither meat-eating nor vegetarianism, as there are many of both in our ranks.

We do most emphatically maintain that spirituality does not come through the stomach; it comes from thought and aspiration and spiritual unfoldment. In all subjects we permit each individual to be a law unto himself. Therefore, we will not take the time to go into the special matters you find so objectionable. We will only reiterate that which we say so constantly and continually in all our works:—take out of them that which you find helpful, but permit others to do the same. And do not try to force your own decision universally upon all, or make every Soul measure up to your own standards. It is most important that each shall decide for himself, not what food will bring him spirituality but what will bring him the greatest health and vitality and thus enable him to live a helpful life for the world and unfold love and tolerance. As we said before, spirituality does not come because of what we do or do not eat.

We have a little grace which we advise oar students to say before meals. "I am a creator. By the power of my spiritualized will I consciously gather all the forces from this food and use them to create health, strength and harmony in all my bodies." The idea is that the body should take care of any wholesome food we give it.

> "However much I shrink from violence, and fear for those I love, my voice will be the last to condemn the Communists when they overthrow the mammonizing governments of the modern world."
>
> March 15, 1923.

As to "condemnation of the mammonized governments," we must endeavor to refrain from all condemnation; instead we must pray earnestly that the right and proper guidance for humanity will find someone to express it. There is a law which has always manifested in this world that the power of government shifts in cycles according to man's thoughts, hence man is responsible for the kind of government he permits. At first man was governed by the Divine Masters of Truth and Wisdom, or let us say by Divine Rulers. These Divine Rulers were truly kings—kings "by divine right,"—because they had learned to rule, first themselves, and then the forces of the Earth. They were crowned, not by a man-made crown, but by a crown of radiant spiritual emanations, or crown of glory, so that all mankind recognized their divine right to rule and gladly sought their guidance. But after certain cycles had elapsed and mankind had grown up and been taught the principles of true government, it had to learn to put those principles into practice for itself. So ultimately the Divine Rulers withdrew to take up Their work in the higher realms, leaving behind certain chosen human disciples (priests) as their representatives.

This chosen Priesthood is able to rule with justice and equity as long as it is in conscious touch with the Divine Rulers. But gradually this God-inspired rulership degenerates into mere priestcraft. Then the rulership is seized by the military caste which rules through force, fear and cruelty. Thus ultimately Church and State are separated. But since such rulers cannot carry out their personal ambitions and selfish schemes without great financial resources, after a long time a cycle is entered wherein the real rulership is in the hands of the financiers—or "big business," as in the wars of recent years. The rule of "big business" is destined to be followed by the rule of the people, the masses, whether through republics, democracies or some proletarian form, each form or cycle of rulership overlapping the other for long periods. But ultimately humanity will find that wisdom does not lie in mere numbers; that no multiplication of ignorance can produce wisdom; that even the best of the most enlightened human wisdom is lacking, and that some form of Divine Guidance is necessary, or rulership based on eternal *spiritual principles* instead of human desires and expediency. Then mankind will again turn to the Divine for guidance when they have had enough of both extremes—inherited wealth and power or ignorance and inefficiency—and seek divinely illuminated Kings once more chosen because of their conscious touch with the Divine, being both priests and kings, to rule over them during the more spiritual age to come.

At the present time the world is being largely governed by "big business" and the real rulers are those who can get the most money. But we must realize that the real ruler of the people is always the condensed, united force of the people's thoughts and desires, so we should seek to condemn in ourselves that which desires any kind of rulership of the merely physical, and should ask that the Divine only shall rule us and manifest through us. Then are we throwing our force toward the divine rulership of those who will be real kings, because of their Divine Power and their desire for the good of the people over whom they are ruling. Then, and only then, will we bring the world around to the right standards of government.

Only to a certain extent is "all well with the world because God is in his heaven." God must also be in the hearts of men before all is well. It is our duty to take upon ourselves a full understanding of the trend of the times, for remember this, that the trend of the times is the trend of humanity's heart-love and desire. And everyone who seeks to make this heart-love a positive thing and to let it be known that he desires good and only good, is spreading it. For all things, even evil, have their auric manifestations and spread out from the consciousness of humanity in all directions. Since this is the planet of man's free-will and testing, here he must choose to be good of his own free-will. Good is ultimately much stronger than evil and if we will let the Lord Christ enter into our consciousness and radiate from us, we will be accomplishing for the good of all humanity.

> "Will it ever be possible for me to know and realize, and to be conscious of the state of existence that I am in or where I am on the Path of attainment? I cannot tell whether I am even on the Path or not, altho I have been studying for 20 years."
>
> Sept.12, 1922.

You need not waste time wondering about where you are on the Path, but just go on. For there are

Miscellaneous

so many things that interblend on the Path; for instance, we must meet and conquer many various things, all of which have their part as steps on the Path. We may find ourselves far ahead in the overcoming of some things and so might judge ourselves at a certain gate or stopping place; yet later we might find that in some other point of overcoming we were lacking, which would again put us back.

When the time comes for you to know just where you stand in your spiritual unfoldment and development, it will be given to you: not by any mortal nor even by any spiritual advanced Teacher, but by the Lord Christ himself, who will speak to you in the Silence and tell you.

So, instead of trying to locate definitely where you are on the Path, look rather to the things in yourself that you know you have not conquered and strive to conquer them. For, on the Path we should take up our burden of life or our personality and determine to carry it to the feet of the Christ and there ask the Living Christ to help us to conquer it. Nor do we reach any definite step until we have truly overcome our most besetting sins. One of the most difficult parts of the Path, which goes with us practically all the way, is the ability to look deeply into our own personal life and unflinchingly recognize our own shortcomings and to try, through the power of the Christ within us, to transmute them into good.

All that any of us need to know is that we are facing such and such conditions and that we would not be facing them were they not necessary for our unfoldment. We do not have to know just what part of the Path we are on, but should say: "I know the strength is ready and waiting for me to conquer this thing," or let us say, to take this next step on the Path. Have faith and hold fast to the hand of the loving Christ and rest in the absolute understanding that whatever comes is best because it is your place and the place where you can overcome the hard conditions and learn their lessons.

APPENDIX

A PRAYER FOR WORLD HARMONY[1]

"One woe is past; and, behold, there come two woes more hereafter." *Revelation*, ix, 12.

"From the present outlook (1921) of world conditions we may calculate that the first period of readjustment, "an hour," will see the readjustment of capital and labor, *which is quite likely to come to a tremendous crisis soon* . . . .the second phase, "a day" may well be the struggle for the political and social readjustments now taking place . . . .The third phase, "a month," will embrace the great upheaval and consequent strife and struggle which is unavoidable in the overturning and readjustment of religious conceptions, teachings and thoughts on spiritual subjects." *The Message of Aquaria*, Curtiss, 242-3.

The whole world is today passing through a dense smothering cloud of karmic[2] dust which has accumulated through ages of wrong thinking and acting, wrong conceptions of the Law of Life. And, alas, many are letting this dust so blind the eyes of their understanding that they believe that only through extreme selfishness, retaliation and revenge can they end their injustice and suffering; that only as the Earth is drenched with the blood of their fellow men can peace, brotherhood, justice and prosperity reign. This idea is being so systematically propagated among the unthinking masses that unless some positive effort is made by those who know the Law of Life (harmony and co-operation), those who see and feel and know that all such separative and destructive ideas will only result in a prolongation of the same conditions from which mankind has suffered so long, together with all those who desire better conditions, all united in a persistent effort to make a firm stand on the principles of harmony and interdependence, which we see exemplified among the various organs of our bodies, the world is destined to rehearse once more the terrible drama of destruction, death and suffering

---

[1] For a fuller discussion see *Coming World Changes*, Curtiss, Chapter VII.
[2] *Karma*, the law of Cause and Effect.

unspeakable which it has already passed through in so many previous cyclic periods of revolution inaugurated in the name of freedom and reform. Since man's material evolution has steadily increased his ability to intensify the punishment he metes out to his brother man—and hence ultimately to himself—in the name of "brotherhood," and since the very dust of the Earth cries out, "How long, O Lord, how long?" we call upon all well-wishers of humanity throughout the world, especially those who are beginning to sense the chill breath of the coming terror, to unite with us to "lift up their gates" and let in the King of Glory, that through the outshining of His radiance they may have power to help transmute the clouds of inharmony now hanging over mankind and avert the disasters which otherwise will naturally follow; for conditions never right themselves, they are righted only through the *definite constructive* action of certain persons or groups of persons who understand and unite to work wisely toward definite ends.

Firstly, we must systematically spread the idea that it is *wrong principles* and *rules of life* we are to combat, not persons or peoples; that we cannot reform another person or nation until we have carefully searched in our own hearts and in our own nation for our faults and have recognized and shown a willingness to correct them. We must also continually spread the idea that force, coercion, revenge, hatred, cruelty, even the repetition of and clinging to the memory of wrongs we have suffered, are destructive forces which can only add to and never heal the wounds from which all the world is groaning together today.

The first to work definitely with the Spiritual Powers which are seeking to lift up the gates of ignorance and inculcate the constructive principles of the Law of Life should be those advanced students whose consciousness can grasp and realize this Law and its applications, as they have been set forth by this Order in the wide scope and variety of its philosophical and spiritual Teachings. Just as during the Great War we were the first to inaugurate a world-wide daily Noon Prayer-service for the triumph of right and justice, which we feel had a great psychological effect in shortening the days of carnage—for it was largely a psychological breakdown or loss of morale which brought the war to such a sudden end—so we again today ask our students in all parts of the world, together with all their friends who are willing to join with them, to repeat morning, noon and night, or oftener, but at least at noon each day, the following *Prayer for World Harmony* with a deep heart-felt realization of its significance and a scientific understanding of its dynamic psychological power to awaken *and stimulate into action* every germ of good in the hearts of mankind—the love, the compassion, the justice, co-operation and all constructive forces, and thus neutralize and transmute the evil—that the terrible rising tide of unrest, selfishness, racial and class antagonism, labor troubles and religious bigotry and intolerance, among individuals, classes and nations, may be so transmuted, or at least turned aside, that it will not find expression in a new series of armed conflicts and bloodshed.

The uniting of thousands of hearts and minds to this definite end should generate a great current of dynamic spiritual force sweeping continuously around the world—for it is noon somewhere every minute of the day—which like a refreshing breeze should cool the heat of conflicting interests and blow off the karmic dust of the past which is settling upon and blinding individuals and nations to the Law of Life, harmony and co-operation. Thus shall we be of practical psychological help in opening wide "the everlasting doors" and preparing for the quick coming of the King of Glory, not only into our own hearts and lives, but into the lives of nations and humanity as a whole.

Remember that the battle which is still raging in the world is a battle of principles, and that the Law of Life must ultimately prevail. But it will prevail only after terrible calamities and renewed suffering to individuals, classes and nations *unless they unite* to lift up their gates and permit the King of Glory to come in and help them transmute the clouds of karmic dust and inharmony into peace, brotherhood and co-operation.

See the Radiance which this Prayer invokes, dispelling the clouds of inharmony as the Sun dispels the fog, and stimulating the growth of the good in each heart as the Sun stimulates the growth of the sprout when the fog has been dispelled and the Sun can carry on its constructive work.

PRAYER FOR WORLD HARMONY

Glory and honor and worship be unto Thee, O Lord Christ,
  Thou who art the Life and Light of all mankind!
Thou art the King of Glory to whom all the peoples of the
  Earth should give joyful allegiance and service.
Inspire mankind with a realization of true Brotherhood.
Teach us the wisdom of peace, harmony and co-operation.
Breathe into our hearts the understanding that only as we see
  ourselves as parts of the one body of humanity can peace,
  harmony, success and plenty descend upon us.
Help us to conquer all manifestations of inharmony and evil
  in ourselves and in the world.
Bless us all with the Radiance of Thy Divine Love and
  Wisdom that we may ever worship Thee in the beauty of
  holiness.
In the Name of the Living Christ we ask it. Amen.

Prayer for Light

  O Christ! Light Thou within my heart
  The Flame of Divine Love and Wisdom,
  That I may dwell forever in the radiance of Thy countenance
  And rest in the Light of Thy smile!

Morning Prayer

  I have within me the power of the Christ!
  I can conquer all that comes to me today!
  I am strong enough to bear every trial
  And accept every joy
  And to say
  Thy will be done!

Healing Prayer

O thou loving and helpful Master Jesus!
Thou who gavest to Thy disciples power to heal the sick!
We, recognizing Thee, and realizing Thy divine Presence
  with us,
Ask Thee to lay Thy hands (powers) upon us in healing
  Love.
Cleanse US from all OUR sins, and by the divine power of
  Omnipotent Life,
Drive out the atoms of inharmony and disease, and
Fill our bodies full to overflowing with Life and Love and
  Purity.

Prayer of Protection

O Christ! Surround and fill me and Thy Order with the
  Flame of Divine Love and Wisdom,
That it may purify, illumine and guide us in all things.
May its Spiritual Fire form a rampart of Living Flame
  around me and Thy Order
To protect us from all harm.
May it radiate to every heart, consuming all evil and
  intensifying all good
In the name of the Living Christ! Amen.

Prayer of Demonstration

I am a child of the Living God!
I have within me the all-creating power of the Christ!
It radiates from me and blesses all I contact.
It is my Health, my Strength, my Courage,
My Patience, my Peace, my Poise,
My Power, my Wisdom, my Understanding,
My Joy, my Inspiration, and my Abundant Supply.
Unto this great Power I entrust all my problems,
Knowing they will be solved in Love and Justice.
(Mention all problems connected with your worldly affairs,
  visualize each and conclude with the following words)
O Lord Christ! I have laid upon Thy altar all my wants and
  desires.
I know Thy Love, Thy Wisdom, Thy Power and Thy Graciousness.
In Thee I peacefully rest, knowing that all is well.
For Thy will is my will. Amen.

Prayer to the Divine Indweller

Come, O Lord of Life and Love and Beauty!
Thou who art myself and yet art God!
And dwell in this body of flesh.
Radiating all the beauty and holiness and perfection,
That the flesh may out-picture all that Thou art within!
Even so come, O Lord. Amen.

Prayer to the Divine Mother

O Divine Mother!
Illumine me with Divine Wisdom,
Vivify me with Divine Life and
Purify me with Divine Love,
That in all I think and say and do
I may be more and more Thy child. Amen.

Grace at Meals

I am a creator.
By the power of my spiritualized will I consciously gather all the forces from this food, and use them to create health, strength and harmony in all my bodies (physical, astral and mental).

Sunset Prayer

As the physical sun
Disappears from our sight,
May the Spiritual Sun
Arise in our hearts,
Illumine our minds,
And shed its radiant blessing
Upon all we contact.

INDEX

A
Abortion, 147; reasons, 150
Affinities, 180-1
Affirmations, 10
America, disasters, 49, 51; great Temple in, 50; Karma, 49; new race in, 232; opportunity of, 52
Astral, body, 28; entities, 23-4; protection against, 24, 29; teachings from, 24; traveling in, 29
Autopsy, 90
Avatar, 198, 203-7-8-10; alike, 215-19

B
Baptism, 210-11
Behemoth, 164
Bible, how written, 119-215; inspired, 76, 118; interpretation, 204; symbology, 230
Bisson, Mme., 21
Body, do not despise, 84-5-6; expresses inheritances, 9; fire, 224
Bolshevist, 138

C
Celibacy, 160, 179
Cells, 19
Challenge, 26, 31, 95, 113, 120
Changes, coming world, 48; prearranged, 51
Christ, Consciousness, 204-10-11-16; Cosmic, 202, 218; in herbs, 18; Principle, 199, 200; soon to come, 56, 208; Sun and, 199
Claims, make no, 61, 78
Clairvoyance, 28
Communications, 110; automatic, 114, 120-1; with Masters, 115-6
Communion, with dead, 34, 95, 100, 110-11-12, 120, 143; with suicide, 97
Communism, 234
Convents, 62
Co-operation, 55-6-7; of societies, 71-2
Concentration, 39
Cremation, 88
Crucifixion, 207-9, 212

D
David, House of, 232
Death, after, 88-9; animals after, 102; fighting, 95; forgiveness, 99; held after, 93-4; in infancy, 147, 151; meeting after, 99; sleep after, 100
Dementia Praecox, 13
Demonstrations, 126, 205
Diet, 16, 133
Disasters, America and, 49, 52; details, 48; effects of, 54; fear not, 49, 51; like Sodom, 56; many due, 56; those killed in, 49; to prevent, 55, 92
Discouragement, 189
Discretion, 76
Disease, acute, 12; bacterial, 12; functional, 12
Divorce, 167-8, 181
Dogmas, before, 214; curse 157
Drink habit, 30
Duality, Law of, 170-1
Duty, in world, 62-3; to family, 61; to self, 194
Dweller, on Threshold, 230

E
Earth, cures, 17
Ecstasy, 108
Embalming, 89
Emotions, higher, 105-8
Europe conditions in, 54-7

F
Family, world a, 55
Fasting, 15, 16, 85
Faults, facing, 71
Finances, 122
Fishes, two, 227
Food, spiritual, 66
Founders, chosen, 77; transmitters, 78
Funeral, ordeal, 89

G
Geley, Prof. Gustave, 21
Gifts, God's, 141
Gnostics, 215
Grace, before meals, 16, 234
Guidance, Divine, 65, 83

H

Habits, 79
Healing, broadcasted, 14; herbs, 17; instantaneous, 11, 13; our method, 12, 15, 33; prayer, 14
Health, examination needed, 7, 10, 13, 192; use scientific methods, 10, 18
Heaven, 40-1
Hell, 40-1
Helpers, invisible, 88, 92, 192
Herbs, 17
Hunting, 228

I

Ideal, invisible, 20
Illness, 11
Immaculate, 220
Initiation, 225
Inspiration, 75, 81, 118
Interpretation, Symbolic, iii, 204, 230

J

Jesus, and the Christ, 198, 201; appearance of, 203; blessing of, 202-3; not mortal, 210-11-12; our teaching on, 206-7-12; story of, 198, 203-4-6-7, 212-15; thinking you are, 214; was weak, 214
Joseph, 198, 217, 231

K

Karma, Law of, 35, 117; assumed, 47; family, 149; financial. 131-2; governs incarnation, 143-4; invoking, 36, 41; Lords of, 34; marriage and, 179, 180; not fate, 38; not punishment, 42; of America, 49; of personality, 43; of Soul, 43-7; of two lives, 43; race, 50-5; sex and, 183; wheel of, 84
Kings, divine right of, 234

L

Leaves, putting forth, 191
Lessons, of Earth, 99, 142-4-9, 163-9, 172
Leviathan, 164
Life, after death, 21; clinging to, 40; not from cells, 19; Principle, 20
Loaves, five, 227
Luck, no, 133, 168

M

Marriage, astrology and, 178; between races, 185; divorce and, 177; guidance for, 177; holy, 29, 177; Karma and, 179; object of, 153; only love sanctions, 166; quarrels, 187; spiritual, 151; vows, 165-7; without intercourse, 176
Man, the Divine, 200
Mary, 219
Masters, K. H., 115; laws of, 183; teachings from, 61, 118; touch with, 73, 115-6; without wealth; 129, 130
Metals, in body, 12
Mind, cultivate, 195; dual, 10; Higher, 10, 126-7; not adequate, 128; rational, 10; Spiritual, 10
Monasteries, 62, 136

N

Nature, 82-3, 154
Nirmanakaya, 224
Notzing, Dr. von Schrenk, 21

O

Obsession, 21, 111-3; alcoholic, 30 -1; of a society, 35
Operations, 8, 9
O. C. M., claims, 68, 73-4-5-8; leaves all free, 58; not an organization, 60; requirements of, 70-1; teachings, 61-2-3, 75, 84, 223; tolerant, 64; work of, 59, 63
Ouija board, 112-3

P

Path, the, 70, 336; hard, 190; of Renunciation, 87; of Service, 87; to Mastery, 208
Phenomena, 32
Planchette, 111-2-3
Pledges, Karma of, 59; to personalities, 42, 70
Poverty, vows of, 124-5
Prayer, 103; answered, 22, 133-5; Develop in me, 128; for children, 109; object of, 107; of Three Doors, 7, 109, 190; of Four Angels, 109; of the Order, appendix; use of, 10, 17, 18, 103; words and, 106
Prevision, 28
Profits, 137-8
Protection, Ring of, 95
Psychic, chills, 29, 30; conditions, 23; powers, 92; sensations, 28; terror, 24
Puberty, 148
Punishment, Karma not, 42; no, 49, 158, 180
Purity, 159, 160-3

R

Races, early, 174
Radio, mental, 81
Reincarnation, 40-1-6, 63, 91, 117, 142; as nun, 151-2; immediate, 151; Karma and, 143-4-9; object of, 86, 148, 178; of families, 143; on other planets, 163; Soul chooses, 150; time between, 143; time for, 148; telling of past, 145, 182; why denied, 144
Religion, a world, 224; fashions in, iv; Wisdom not limited, 61, 81; restatement of, 60
Rulership, 234-5

S

St. Paul, 158
Salt, kinds, 12; use, 18
Seed, 65-7; pattern in, 226
Self, Divine, 9; emotions from, 105
Sex, change of, 171-2-3, 182; Law of Nature, 175-6; lessons of, 145; not evil, 154-9, 165, 176; of Soul, 146, 170-1; problem, 153-9, 161-9; separation of, 164, 174; transmutation of, 155-6
Sin, born in, 179; forgiveness of, 221-2
Smoking, 79
Soul, chooses family, 150; descent of, 26; feminine, 146, 182; home, 74-8, 171; in astral, 171; mates, 154, 167, 178, 180-1; mission of, 85: saving one's, 62; sex of, 146, 170-1-3; takes possession, 148, 200; twin, 184
Spiritualism, 32-4
Spirituality, 16
Sub-conscious, mind, 29; takes suggestions, 8, 191
Suffragettes, 173
Suicide, 96-7-8

Sun, in Nature, 193-9, 212-16; myth, 218-20; Spiritual, 67, 193
Swine, 77

T

Teacher, appears, 63-4; personal, 82
Teachings, East vs. West, 83-4; introduced by H. P. B., 77-8; more than human, 77; object of, 84; source of, 80; support of, 140; without price, 139
Tears, 195
Teeth, 13, 192
Thought, 126, 157, 179
Tissues, kept alive, 20
Tolerance, 55; of Order, 80
Transmutation, 155-6
Tribes, lost, 230-1
Truth, ridiculed, iii

U

Universe, Builders of the, 58-9

V

Vegetarians, 233
Violin, 135
Vows, Karma of, 59; marriage, 165-7; not required, 58; of poverty, 124-5

W

War, in Europe, 57
Water of Life, 61
Wealth, misuse of, 131; use of, 123-4, 131; withheld, 129, 130
Words, use of, 106-7
Workers, selected, 51-2, 77
Working man, 138
Worm, 226
Worry, 45, 100
Writing, automatic, 114, 120-1; inspirational, 121

X

X-ray, use of, 13, 14

Z

Zodiac, 178, 231

www.ingramcontent.com/pod-product-compliance
Lightning Source LLC
Chambersburg PA
CBHW061635040426
42446CB00010B/1430